LONGEVITY

The Chinese Secret to a
Long and Happy Life

MIKE VESTIL

TABLE OF CONTENTS

A NOTE FOR YOU, THE READER

Thank you for picking up this book. Taking care of health and youthfulness is not always easy. Life gets busy, stress piles up, and it's easy to forget the simple things that make the biggest difference. That's why I wanted to create something that feels like a companion, not just a book.

As a small gift for reading, you can download a free companion tool kit here: **mikevestil.com/longevity-gifts**

(or scan the QR code below)

SCAN ME

Inside, you'll find:

➤ **Stress to Stillness Checklist:** A simple daily guide to move from tension to peace. Each step helps you release mental clutter, ground your body, and return to a state of calm focus.

➤ **The *Qi* Flow Tracker:** A mindful daily log that connects breath, movement, food, emotions, and rest to help you notice what truly fuels or drains your life force.

➤ **The Morning Ritual Journal:** A morning reflection journal template to center your energy, set your intention, and begin your day with purpose, balance, and quiet strength.

➤ **The Evening Return Journal:** A nightly journaling ritual to release the day, restore peace in your body, and invite deep, healing sleep.

These are the same kinds of practices I wish I had been given earlier: small, practical steps that make staying youthful feel simple and even joyful. My hope is that these tools walk with you as gentle reminders that health, peace, and longevity are built one day at a time.

INTRODUCTION:

THE DAY I LEARNED I WOULD DIE

I remember the first time I learned I was going to die. I was five years old, sitting in the back of our brown Honda Civic, the one that smelled like old coffee cups, takeout containers, and the slow tiredness of immigrant dreams. My legs were kicking like little legs do when they can't reach the floor, dressed in purple corduroy overalls that my mom had picked out. They made me feel like a stuffed toy: cute, stiff, not entirely mine. I didn't know how to use words like "claustrophobic" or "existential," but I remember the weight in my chest. The air was warm and Midwestern, sticky with humidity, thick with the smell of freshly cut grass at a baseball field and fresh tar. We had just left a funeral.

I don't recall how I felt at the funeral, as it was my first time attending one. I was confused about why everyone looked so sad. I just remember that we had driven through the baseball field near our church, the same route we always took. We passed the chain-link fences and empty bleachers. My sister was in the car seat beside me, a one-year-old, her nose running, her mouth wet with drool, making soft baby sounds, while the rest of us were heavy in silence. I rolled the window down, stuck my hand out like a paper plane, catching the

3

wind. I imagined myself as a superhero, flying above the roads and fields, untouchable and free. The wind felt cool between my fingers. My fingers felt real. I felt alive.

I looked over at my sister, then back at the front of the car, and asked the question no one was ready for.

"Dad, where did Uncle go?"

My dad didn't answer right away. He was gripping the wheel with that kind of tension I would later learn meant *I don't know how to talk about this*. After a long pause, he looked at me through the rearview mirror. His eyes were tired and heavy. He had that permanent crease between his eyebrows even back then, like worry had set up camp and never left.

With a voice flat and serious, he said, "Son, he died." I blinked. The words didn't land.

"What does died mean?" I asked.

My dad exhaled again. I can still remember the sound. The sigh wasn't just air; it was the weight of everything he couldn't explain, packed into a single breath.

"It means he's gone," he said. "We'll never see him again." The car kept moving, but something inside me stopped.

"Where did he go?"

My dad answered as if it were a fact. "We had to put him in the ground. He's no longer living."

I didn't fully understand, but I felt something. A fluttering in my belly. A fog in my mind. The kind of confusion that isn't just about words; it's about realizing that the world is bigger and scarier than you knew yesterday. I turned to my mom, her soft Filipino accent like a balm over the rawness of my dad's bluntness. "Baby," she said, "you know the feeling when you go to sleep?"

I nodded, not sure where this was going. "It's like that, but you don't wake up." The car went silent after that. Even my baby sister stopped making sounds. That was the moment the first fear crept into my body. Not the kind of fear that makes you scream or run, but the quiet one that lives in your bones, the kind that changes you.

"So... Uncle just went to sleep and didn't wake up?"

My dad responded, "That's just what happens when you get old. You get sick. You get weak. Then you're gone."

Then came the question I didn't know I was terrified to ask. "So... I'll never see Uncle again?"

They didn't answer right away. They looked at each other. Another long sigh. Then they said the hardest thing a parent has to say to a child. "Yes. Never again."

I began crying. It wasn't like a tantrum, not like a child who didn't get what he wanted. It was more like someone who had just tasted the shape of grief for the first time. That was the moment I became conscious, I think. Not just awake, but aware that everything I loved could be taken from me. I realized nothing was guaranteed, and that life had an end. The tears wouldn't stop. I whispered the next question, "Mom... Dad... will you die one day?"

They froze. I could see their eyes in the mirror. That moment felt like a movie scene, only no one said "cut." Just silence. The sound of tires on the road. The heavy hum of existence between us. Finally, my mom turned around and reached for my hand.

"Yes, dear," she said. "One day, we'll be gone, too."

That's when the crying turned into a storm. It wasn't just sadness; it was terror. My parents? Gone? How would I live? Who would hold me? What would happen to me when they weren't here? I started wailing. My sister started wailing too, just because I was crying. My mom unbuckled herself, turned around, and pulled me into her arms.

"There, there, sweetie," she whispered. "There, there."

She held me like only mothers can. It was like she could stop the world from ending just by keeping my head against her chest. But even in her arms, I whispered, "Mom... will I die, too?" Another long pause.

"Yes, son. We all do."

That moment never left me. It buried itself inside, like a seed of fear. From that day forward, I started watching everything with different eyes. I watched the people I loved get older. I watched the clock more closely. I started wondering how long everything had left. By the time I was eleven, I had become obsessed with health. Not because I was trying to live, but because I was trying not to die.

I still remember the day I learned what sugar could do to the body. It was in biology class. I was the nerdy kid, always raising my hand and finishing the readings early. The one who sat in the front row and never got in trouble. I wanted to be a doctor, a dentist, or a nurse. Not because I wanted to help people, but because that's what Filipino kids are raised to be: white-coat professionals who send money back home and make their parents proud.

We were learning about glucose and insulin, and I remember the textbook saying something like, "Too much sugar over time can lead to blindness, nerve damage, heart disease." I didn't finish reading the rest. I just stopped at "blindness."

Blindness meant weakness. Weakness meant death. I slammed the book shut. That night, I didn't have dessert. I skipped the waffles the next morning. I poured the apple juice down the drain. Before, every single waffle square was filled to the top with syrup. Now, even the smell of sugar made me feel sick.

One by one, I began cutting out foods. First sugar, then fat, then oils, then meats, then rice. I became a self-imposed nutrition monk, lacking wisdom and balance. I believed that if I controlled everything I consumed, I could delay death or maybe even escape it.

By the time I was fifteen, I was underweight, pale, and anxious. I looked like a cartoon character with a big head and a pencil-drawn body. Inside, I was worse. My stomach was always in knots. My skin felt too thin. My fear had eaten more of me than any disease could have.

When I got older, the fear didn't go away. It just changed shape. In college, death didn't feel far away anymore. It felt close. Like it was slowly showing up in the people I loved. Every time I visited home, I noticed something different in my parents. My mom's hair getting whiter. The laugh lines around her eyes deepening into trenches. My dad's belly growing rounder. His face puffier. His steps slower.

It hit me all over again: they were really going to die. Maybe not tomorrow or next year, but one day. And every day brought them closer. Worse than the fear was the guilt that perhaps I was the reason they were aging faster, draining them. Their sacrifice of working long hours, paying bills, and sending me to dental school was shaving years off their lives. All so I could chase a dream that wasn't mine.

My dad would wake up at 3 a.m. every day to catch the train to work. My mom at 5 a.m., her lunch packed in Tupperware. They passed each other like ghosts, tag-teaming exhaustion just to keep the lights on and the dream alive. But the dream wasn't mine. Dental school was never mine. I left it behind. Not peacefully. Not with a planned, mature exit. I left like a storm. I booked a one-way flight to Asia and disappeared from the life they had built for me.

They were crushed, confused, and angry. My mom cried every day for a week. My dad didn't talk to me for a month. But beneath the hurt, I believe they also felt some relief. Because maybe, finally, I was choosing to live. That's when everything changed.

In a dusty town in Asia, somewhere between rice terraces and temple bells, I discovered something that would change the rest of my life. It was a Chinese concept I had never heard of before. It was a quiet secret passed down through families who had been living, smiling, and thriving into their nineties and beyond.

I didn't know it at the time, but I was about to unlearn everything I thought I knew about longevity. Not just how not to die, but how to truly live. With joy. With energy. With time. The secret was simple, yet everything I had been missing. That story of what I found, and how it gave me more years with my mom and dad, is what this book is about.

One day, my daughter will look up at me and ask, "Dad, what is death?"

Instead of fumbling in the dark, instead of offering fear disguised as comfort, I'll pull her close and whisper, "Baby girl, let me tell you the story of the first time I learned I was going to die, and how I learned to live instead."

I'll tell her how her grandma, who once looked like life had worn her down, now seems to be aging backwards, with glowing skin and laughter in her eyes, no longer burdened by her body. I'll tell her how her grandpa, whose knees once cracked with every step, can now drop and do twenty push-ups at seventy-two because he wants to, not because he needs to prove anything. I'll tell her that aging isn't the enemy. And I'll tell her the truth: that most of us don't fear death. We fear not having lived. That's what this book is for.

To remember. To reclaim. To return.

To share a few secrets not from billion-dollar labs or pharmaceutical companies, but from grandmothers in Chinese mountain villages, from old men practicing *tai chi* at dawn, from herbalists who still believe in *Qi*, and from families who still gather around round tables, slurping soup and laughing together without a clock in sight.

This book is not a manual. It is not a prescription. It is a love letter to the body you live in, to the time you've been given, and to the ones you hope never to say goodbye to. So if you've ever looked in the mirror and wondered where your youth went, if you've ever looked at your parents and prayed for more years, or if you've ever tasted the fear of finality and wished for a second chance at life, I invite you to turn the page. Because what you'll find isn't just how to look young or stay young, but how to live young. With joy. With connection. With peace.

Until your last breath... and beyond.

CHAPTER 1

Qi

(氣)

LIFE, ENERGY, AND BALANCE

I couldn't poop, and it scared the hell out of me.

Now, I know. It sounds ridiculous. Comedic. Something you'd toss out as a punchline over beers with friends. But in that moment, hunched over in a cramped bathroom in Asia, knees pressed against the tile, sweat clinging to the back of my neck, it wasn't funny. It was terrifying. Not because I thought I was going to die, but because for the first time, I realized something inside me was stuck. And it wasn't just the poop.

A friend of mine once looked at me, observing the life I had begun to build, the businesses, the decision to leave dental school, and the shift into something I hoped would bring security to my mom and dad as they grew older. One day, he asked, "Mike, what do you think success really looks like?"

Without hesitation, I looked him straight in the eye, kept my face blank as stone, and said, "A smooth, effortless poop every single day."

He laughed. I didn't.

"You're serious?"

"Dead serious."

He thought I was being philosophical, maybe even cheeky, but I wasn't. I was speaking from the pit of my gut, or maybe more accurately, from the stubborn block that had made its home there. Because somewhere between chasing gurus and chasing goals, I had stopped flowing. The body doesn't lie. And mine had been whispering to me for years. That day, it finally screamed.

I didn't have words for it then, but what I was feeling was the collapse of *Qi (chee)*, the life force that animates not just our breath, but our rhythm, hunger, aging, sleep, grief, orgasms, and dreams. When *Qi* is moving, you feel alive. When it stagnates, you decay while still breathing.

I was slowly falling apart. The pressure of escaping my insecurities, juggling work responsibilities, and managing family expectations, all while maintaining the façade of being the "good son" and the "strong one" in our family, became overwhelming. It felt like everything was held together by a thin string that was fraying at both ends, ready to snap under the weight of the constant negative thoughts that plagued my anxious mind. I tried to sleep away my worries and troubles, but I kept waking up at 3:17 a.m., staring at the clock until dawn, only to realize that my sleep was ruined yet again by anxiety. From the outside, it appeared that I had everything figured out; on the inside, I was collapsing.

For example, I remember sitting alone at home one day, in my insecurities, feeling like I wasn't enough, feeling like I wasn't good enough, constantly thinking, *damn, why couldn't I have been born like that person? Am I in the right career?* There would be constant anger and hatred directed towards myself. So that anger essentially created this need to chase these gurus, who I thought essentially would have the answer. Because a lot of my insecurities were in my body.

I was made fun of as a kid because they said I was too skinny. A lot of the kids when I was younger were racist to me because I was the kid that my friends would just, for some reason, forget to invite. These insecurities really honed in on me, really had me trying to chase success and a better body to essentially hide the insecurities that lay in my heart. So I chased it. A lot of this was really about success. I chased success because people told me it's all about hustling, grinding, and making more money. You can sleep when you're dead.

And I chased that, but it left me burnt out, barely seeing my family, struggling with stress, constantly comparing my finances to others, and always feeling insecure. It only increased my anxiety as I pursued success. With health, it was always the same; I would try to achieve my dream body as quickly as possible, but it often led to injuries. While living in Bali, I tried being a vegan for a while because some vegan coach told me it would change my life, and I found out it really messed up my gut. Then I tried keto or carnivore diets, trying the opposite approach, and it also messed up my gut. I even attempted fasting to the extreme. Again, it messed up my gut.

All the mainstream advice I followed, for some strange reason, made my gut health worse. After years of severe constipation and stomach pain caused by stress from chasing success, fad diets, supplements, workout plans, and a body image I thought would make me feel loved, I now found myself telling my friend that the secret to success is daily poops.

Because as I chased certain extremes, I realized that all extremes eventually lead to burnout, stress, and overwhelm. The location, environment, and the people you surround yourself with will dictate the emotions you feel. The emotions I was feeling were manifesting as a need to control everything and not let go. On a spiritual level, it meant I had no idea "how to trust" or "go with the flow." On a strictly biological level, it meant "I was constipated." Oh, how poetic life is when the body, mind, and spirit are analogies of each other.

So now, I try living in places where I have daily poops because the environment is the most supportive of who you become. And the daily poops are the physical reflection of what my life would look like when I'm spiritually and literally in "the flow."

For example, if the flower doesn't grow, it's not the seed's fault. You just change the soil it grows in. My poop wasn't coming out, so my lifestyle with my career, my finances, and the diets that I chased was not the best environment for me to poop. When my parents retired, we all moved back to our motherland, the Philippines, to delve deeper into my roots. But for some reason, my roots weren't helping me poop.

So I ended up doing the one thing I knew could save me because after getting a colonoscopy before my thirtieth birthday, I saw just how much inflammation and ulcers I had due to GERD (gastroesophageal reflux disease), gastritis, and irritable bowel syndrome caused by being overly stressed, overworked, and exhausted. I ended up flying with my dad and mom to Thailand to stay with my little sister, Angelique, for ten days for her birthday so she could essentially help me with my bowel movements because she works with many health and wellness clients in marketing, branding, and design. And because she has worked with top health and wellness experts, clinicians, and healthcare providers on their branding and website design, she knows all the insights on how to make sure that I poop daily.

Angelique, bless her, was probably the only person on the planet who could help me.

My mom, dad, and I flew to Thailand to visit my sister, who lives in the exact same cozy little village where I first moved when I left America, and we arrived at 12:30 a.m.

She picked us up at the airport, hair tied back, a big smile on her face. I hugged her tightly.

"I missed you," I said.

"I missed you, too," she replied. "Happy early birthday to me."

"Angelique," I said, deadpan. "Please help me poop."

She burst out laughing. "You came all this way for that?"

"Yes."

Her boyfriend, Pete, loaded our bags into the car, and I looked at him with pleading eyes. "You, too, man. I need all the help I can get."

That night, I fell asleep like a baby, dreaming, I kid you not, of soft, cloud-like poop.

The next morning, I naturally woke up at 6 a.m. No alarm. Just the rhythm of my body, trying to find its way back. I wandered downstairs quietly, and what I saw made me stop mid-step. My dad, barefoot and dressed like an old Chinese monk, was moving slowly through the garden. His arms were flowing like water, his wrists turning like silk in a breeze. Palms rotating in slow circles as if he were playing with an invisible koi fish. His breath was deep, effortless. His spine was long. He looked peaceful and centered. The years of stress had softened from his face. At seventy-two, he looked younger than he had in the last decade.

"Good morning," he said without turning, still flowing through his movement.

"Good morning," I replied, blinking slowly, as if I had just walked into a dream.

The movements weren't unfamiliar to me; I had seen them before, years ago in Bali, during a time when my life was falling apart. Back then, I had invited my entire family to visit, hoping to impress them and show that I was okay and capable of taking care of them. I wanted to prove that my business wasn't collapsing, even though, at the time, it truly was. I wanted to convey that I wasn't afraid, even though I was. I didn't want them to know I was sleeping on the floor of a small corner room in a villa that didn't belong to me. I relied on a Chinese friend I barely knew, who was paying most of the rent while pretending that the whole house was mine.

It was all a mask. A beautiful one. And it was heavy.

My Chinese friend, Chang, was a wise, soft-spoken, and always calm human being with a beautiful soul and a larger-than-life body that looked warrior-strong. His hair flowed over his broad shoulders like a Tarzan jungle man, but he had the gentleness and composure of a wise old monk. He introduced me to *qìgōng* and *tai chi* during that time. I was spiraling in anxiety. My gut was a mess. My dad had sciatica so bad that he could barely walk. My mom was worried about everything. My sister, too. So we all gathered on the patio one morning, surrounded by rice fields and golden light, and he taught us how to move.

"No force," he said. "Just follow your breath. Rotate your hips. Imagine your pelvis is a bowl of water. Don't spill it."

We laughed at first. It felt silly.

"Pretend you're holding a fish," he said, showing us the same move my father was now doing that morning in Thailand.

Back then, I rolled my eyes. Now, it made perfect sense.

At that moment, I didn't realize how desperately I needed it. My mind was cluttered, my body tense. My shoulders were always tight, my jaw clenched constantly. I hadn't taken a full breath in what felt like years. But suddenly, something inside me shifted. I sensed heat in my hands, energy flowing down my spine, and a soft hum rising from the ground beneath me. For the first time in a long while, I felt truly present.

And my dad? The same man who once told me, "Just suck it up," during my childhood? He began crying. Not loud sobs, just tears of joy falling silently as his body unwound with each breath and the pressure in his hips and lower back eased from his sciatica.

That was the seed. During the pandemic, when we were all separated due to the lockdowns and travel restrictions of 2020, I was in Bali, my mom in the Philippines, my sister in Thailand, and my dad back in our old home in the Midwest. It was that seed that kept him grounded. While alone, in isolation, in silence, he practiced. Every morning. Slow movements. Deep breath. Flow.

When we reunited after lockdown, I couldn't believe what I saw.

"Dad…" I said, stunned, hugging him. "You look amazing."

He smiled, his cheeks full, his eyes soft. "I've been doing the fish dance."

Now, here we were again. Years after the lockdown. In Thailand. Together. My family. Breathing. Moving. Flowing.

Angelique came down the stairs next, hair still messy but eyes bright. Pete followed, coffee in hand. Without a word, they joined my dad in the garden. My mom stepped out quietly, still half-asleep, and stood beside them. I didn't say anything. I just joined.

No instructions. No teacher. Just memory. Movement. Breath.

There we were, five of us, moving through the morning light like reeds swaying in the wind. Our fingertips traced circles in the air. Our hips rotated gently, warming the spine. Our hearts, after all these years of worry, distance, and survival, beat in a shared rhythm.

That morning, I pooped.

Soft. Effortless. Complete.

It wasn't just a relief. It was a release of all the possessions, comparisons, fears, pursuits, and the need to be someone I wasn't. I sat on the toilet and cried, not from pain, but from gratitude. The next day, I woke up to my dad doing the same dance again. After our morning practice, he shared a story about his childhood friend from China and a parable he had always told my father.

A young man asked an old fisherman, "How do you live so long?"

The fisherman smiled and said, "Each morning, I breathe like the trees and move like the river."

"But what about food? Supplements? Running? Cold plunges?"

The old man laughed. "When your breath flows like wind through bamboo, your blood becomes the sea. What more do you need?"

The young man didn't understand, not until he was old, and found his way back to the sea.

In the West, we fight aging. We resist it with needles, biohacks, ice baths, peptides, stacks, and protocols. We chase youth as if it's something we can buy back. But in the East, youth is not something you chase. It's something you return to.

That's what *Qi* is. It's the unforced, unseen tide of life. It moves when we stop forcing. It rises when we soften. It returns when we listen. We don't "earn" youth. We remove what blocks it: fear, rigidity, excess, comparison, and overthinking.

Qi isn't stored in a supplement. It's stored in your presence. In your breath. In your gut. In the quiet moment you take after the meal, instead of rushing into the next task. In the long walk you take, instead of checking your phone. In the choice to chew slowly, to breathe with intention, to let go instead of clench.

You harness *Qi* not by doing more, but by clearing blockages, not just in the body but in the soul. The fear that tightens your jaw, the pride that stiffens your posture, the comparison that rushes your spirit, the excess that weighs you down, and the overthinking that traps your breath in your chest.

The Chinese have spoken of *Qi* for over 3,000 years, long before microscopes, lab coats, or calorie counts existed. In its earliest form, *Qi* meant "breath" or "steam rising from rice," the invisible essence that provides life with warmth. Daoist sages saw it in the morning mist and the quiet between heartbeats, describing *Qi* as the rhythm of the *Dào* flowing through heaven, earth, and human form. Traditional Chinese Medicine mapped this flow through the body like rivers across a landscape, believing that when *Qi* is blocked, illness occurs. Confucian scholars spoke of righteous *Qi*, a moral energy refined through virtue and discipline. Throughout dynasties, *Qi* remained a sacred current: unseen but always felt. It is not something to conquer, but something to return to.

Qi is vital because everything relies on it. When *Qi* flows, life flows. This includes digestion, immunity, mood, movement, and even your thoughts. When *Qi* is blocked, you notice: unexplained fatigue, emotions you can't explain, aches medicine can't identify. In Traditional Chinese Medicine, health isn't the absence of disease; it's having *Qi* that flows freely through every channel, like a well-irrigated field. *Qi* nourishes your organs, lifts your spirits, and sharpens your senses. Without it, your body slows down, your mind feels chaotic, and your heart feels heavy. It's the difference between just existing and truly thriving, between getting through the day and feeling truly alive. That's why *Qi* is important. When it flows, you do too.

The West didn't always forget *Qi*. It simply called it by other names: vitality, spirit, the soul. But over time, something shifted. As science progressed, anything it couldn't measure was dismissed. The microscope replaced the mirror. Numbers replaced intuition. Healing became surgery. Stillness was equated with laziness. Anything unseen, like *Qi*, was labeled unproven, unprofitable, or unnecessary.

Western medicine began treating symptoms rather than the underlying energy. Muscles, not movement. Organs, not flow. But just because *Qi* can't be bottled doesn't mean it isn't real. You feel it when you're vibrant for no reason. You sense its absence when you're tired, even after rest. The East remembered. The West optimized. Slowly, quietly, we're beginning to remember again.

We cultivate *Qi* not by chasing it, but by honoring the conditions that allow it to rise. Breath is the start... slow, deep, rhythmic. Movement follows. Not frantic workouts, but flowing forms: walking after meals, stretching with the sun, moving like water instead of fire. Food is medicine: warm, cooked, seasonal. Sleep is sacred, aligned with the dark and free from screens. Emotions also matter. Resentment blocks *Qi*, while forgiveness releases it. Gratitude enhances it. Nature restores it. Silence invites it. When life shifts from rushing to rhythm, from pressure to presence, *Qi* begins to grow. Not loudly, but steadily like warmth returning to cold hands.

Morning is the most sacred time to cultivate *Qi* because it's when the world is quiet and your energy is soft, like mist rising from the earth. Before you reach for your phone, reach for your breath. Let it be slow, full, and deep, expanding your belly rather than just your chest. Step outside, even briefly, to greet the light. Stretch your spine, rotate your joints, and walk slowly, barefoot if possible. Drink warm water to start the flow inside. Eat simple, warm foods that are easy to digest and aligned with the seasons. Most importantly, move without rushing. *Qi* gathers in calm. If your first hour is still, the rest of the day will flow smoothly. Cultivating *Qi* in the morning isn't about adding more; it's about starting with less noise, more breath, and a rhythm that respects your life force.

Foods that foster *Qi* are simple, warm, and alive, never processed, extreme, or frozen in plastic. In Traditional Chinese Medicine, *Qi*-rich foods are those prepared gently, easy to digest, and grown in tune with the seasons. Think: congee in the morning, root vegetables in fall, steamed greens, mung beans, sweet potatoes, soft-boiled eggs, broths simmered with care. Whole grains like millet, barley, and rice supply steady energy. Ginger and garlic stimulate circulation. Dates, goji berries, and mushrooms nourish blood and spirit. Cultivating *Qi* isn't about calories; it's about warmth, rhythm, and respect. The more life your food contains, the more life it gives. Eat slowly. Chew thoroughly. And most importantly, eat with peace. A rushed meal, no matter how "healthy," can block more *Qi* than it builds.

Exercises that build *Qi* aren't about exhaustion; they're about circulation, breath, and flow. *Qi* is strengthened through movement that nourishes rather than depletes. *Tai chi, qìgōng*, walking in nature, slow yoga, and even mindful stretching cultivate *Qi* by opening the channels without forcing the body. They sync breath with motion, calm the nervous system, and allow energy to rise like mist over water. Fast, jerky, or overly intense workouts can scatter *Qi* if done too often or without recovery. A gentle morning walk after breakfast, a slow series of movements under the sun, and a deep exhale as you twist and lengthen, build your internal fire without burning you out. Remember, *Qi* flows best when your body feels safe, not strained.

Qi doesn't just come from what you eat or how you move; it's shaped by who you share your breath with. Some people drain you the moment they speak. Others leave you lighter just by being nearby. Spend time with those who exhale peace; people who aren't rushing, performing, or trying to prove themselves. Friends who listen without trying to fix. Elders who speak with warmth, not volume. Children who remind you to laugh. Lovers who don't tense your chest. Seek those who move slowly, eat with gratitude, sleep well, and speak less but with more honesty. *Qi* grows around people who are rooted, not reactive. Calm is contagious. So is chaos. Protect your energy like fire in the wind, and only let those who warm it, not snuff it out, stay close.

This is easier said than done. In the West, it's very simple to work in a stressful environment with toxic people draining your stillness. Maintaining *Qi* in such a setting is an act of quiet rebellion. You don't need to quit your job or escape the noise; you just need to protect your inner calm amid the storm. Start by mastering your breath: slow it down when tension rises, and let your exhale be longer than your inhale. Step away from your desk, even for a minute, and stretch your spine like bamboo swaying in the wind. Drink warm water instead of another coffee. Eat lunch without your phone. Allow silence to settle between tasks. Keep your posture relaxed yet upright. Tension in the shoulders is the first sign *Qi* is leaving. Most importantly, don't let urgency define you. Your presence is your power. In a world fixated on output, peace is your most radical productivity tool.

Under pressure, trying to keep pace with our hectic surroundings, the first thing we lose is our breath. It becomes shallow, quick, trapped in the chest, and with it, our *Qi* starts to scatter. To stay centered when life tightens around you, return to your breath as your anchor. Breathe through your nose, deep into your belly. Slow down the exhale. This signals your body, "I am safe." Inhale for four counts, exhale for six. Pause after the exhale. The space in between is where *Qi* gathers. You can also hum softly. The vibration calms the vagus nerve and steadies the flow of energy. Try "box breathing" (inhale four, hold four, exhale four, hold four) before entering tense spaces. Or trace the breath silently with a mantra like: inhale peace, exhale pressure. Breath is how you hold your ground without fighting. It is softness that doesn't collapse. Power that doesn't shout.

When *Qi* is steady, life flows. You feel it in your skin... warm, bright, awake. You feel it in your gut... calm, intuitive, resilient. Your breath deepens, your mind clears, your posture softens. You don't overreact. You don't overreach. You respond instead of flinching. You rise without forcing. You digest food and emotion with ease. Sleep returns. Libido returns. Laughter returns. *Qi* is not just energy; it's harmony. When your *Qi* is balanced, your body becomes a temple, not a battlefield. Your days feel spacious. Your decisions feel clear. Your presence becomes medicine. This isn't magic. It's rhythm. It's alignment. And it's available, not when you strive, but when you return to what you already are.

When my daughter is old enough to understand how the fast-paced world is designed to drain your *Qi*, this is what I will tell her: Live where you flow. The right environment will do more for your health than any guru ever could. Find the soil that helps your body thrive.

Chase nothing. Flow with everything. Success isn't built on tension; it's built on rhythm, breath, timing, and alignment. Trust your gut... literally. Your body is the first truth-teller. If you're constipated, you're probably clenching somewhere else in life, too.

Move like water. Not to burn calories, but to release what's stuck. Move gently. Move often. Move before you think you need to. Breathe like the trees. Inhale with the sunrise. Exhale with the sunset. Let your breath carry away what your mind can't.

Gather in the morning. Even if just for five minutes, with the people you love. Do the "weird" movements. Laugh. Stretch. Be still.

23

That is family medicine. Don't wait to soften. The world will harden you enough. Be the one who stays gentle.

If one day my daughter finds herself stuck, emotionally, creatively, or physically, I hope she remembers this story. Not because it's about poop, but because it's about life.

Because life, when it is truly alive, flows. And when it flows, it heals. So may your *Qi* move like breath through the trees. May your body remember its song. And may your mornings always begin with movement, family, and ease.

Even if it starts with a poop.

CHAPTER 2

Yǎng Shēng

(養生)

NOURISHING LIFE

———∽m∽———

I fluttered my eyes open and looked up at the ceiling. The weird pinprick holes in the material that made up the hospital ceiling looked old and discarded. I heard beeping to my right, showing that I'd stabilized my heartbeat. I looked at the scrubs I wore. The blue looked overwashed and dried out, and I was covered in a blanket my mom used for long car rides.

Looking at the table, there's a tray of rice and old pork that they feed you in hospitals. Then I looked to my left, where my mom was curled up in a small ball, sleeping in the fetal position, as she had been for the past several days, worried about her son's health. It's been roughly three days since I was admitted to this hospital. It was the closest one to our ancestral area, where my mom and dad were born and raised in the Philippines.

25

Basically, what happened was, three nights before at 11 p.m., I was sitting next to my dad, watching an old kung fu movie on TV, when I suddenly felt unusually weak for someone only twenty-eight. Of course, I didn't want to admit I felt that way. That's just not how men are supposed to act. My dad asked, "Are you fine?"

I said yes. As I nodded my head weakly, we continued watching. Then my mom walked in and asked how I was because I had been complaining to her that I hadn't been feeling well for the past couple of days. She looked at me like a mom does when she's worried and asked, "Are you okay?"

I remember, in that moment, looking at her and being ashamed to admit it, but I just said, "Mom, I feel weak." As I said that, a lot of relief came off my chest as I fully surrendered in realizing that my health was not okay. It was in that moment that she switched from mom to nurse, just as she had when we were in the Midwest before we left America to move to Asia.

She said, "Get in the car, let's go." I weakly walked out the door into the car. I remember curling up in the back seat with the blanket I'm using right now. It was getting late; by the time we arrived at the hospital, it was already midnight.

For some reason, the first two hospitals we went to had emergency rooms that were too busy. My mom, lacking patience, just went to the next one because we couldn't wait. Finally, when we arrived at the emergency room of the third hospital, I heard the sound of medical equipment and people waiting in line, even though it was already 1 a.m. We sat there waiting for a nurse to speak with us. My mom tried to see if she knew anyone, a family friend, as Filipinos often do when they're in unfamiliar areas. She couldn't find any, as they weren't working at the hospital at the time. A younger woman, appearing maybe in her early twenties, who looked like it was her first day on the job, helped us. Her eyes showed the stress of working late-night shifts. Her hair was pulled back, and she wore very big glasses. In the most polite voice, she said, "Ma'am, can I take your son's blood pressure and oxygen?"

She took my blood pressure. I was sitting there trying to pretend to look strong, because I didn't want this girl to see me as weak. She knew I was just wearing a mask. She looked up at my mom and said, "Very weird. His blood pressure is abnormally low." My mom worried a little bit more. "Check his oxygen." She checked my oxygen, 88. I looked at that, knowing it wasn't 99 or 100, like it used to be back when I was healthy. As I saw that number, all the blood left my face. I fainted on the table in the clipboard of that nurse.

When I woke up, I found myself in a hospital bed, changed and dressed, humiliated but aware that I was doing something wrong. I looked at my mom and stayed silent. I wanted her to rest. She didn't deserve to be sleeping in the fetal position on a crooked hospital bench. I then looked out the window, which looked more like a jail cell, and wondered, how did I end up here? I never expected to grow older. I never thought I would face issues like this. I never imagined I could get sick. I didn't think that death would catch up with me so quickly. As I sat there, thinking, rubbing my cheek where the five o'clock shadow I used to shave had turned long, I realized I probably looked like a homeless man wasting away.

The words in my mind told me I wasn't safe. I wasn't good enough. I needed to work harder. I had to hustle. I had responsibilities. I couldn't rest. I needed to suffer to protect my loved ones. I had to make sacrifices to take care of my family. And I knew that voice all too well. That was the voice that pulled me out of the traumatic financial struggles my family faced when I was younger, with Mom and Dad fighting over money, threatening divorce, me acting as the peacemaker and sponge to keep the family together, doing whatever it took to hold it all together, and the drive to work so hard to give them the freedom not to suffer. At first, that was good, but life sometimes swings in the opposite direction. Too much of a good thing can become a bad thing, as I lay in bed, realizing what happens if you let stress, overthinking, anxiety, unspoken depression, and negative spirals go unnoticed for too long.

The funny thing is, I was doing everything right. I was going to the gym consistently. I was taking all my vitamins and supplements. I was biohacking. I was taking my protein. I was eating vegetables. I did everything every health guru told me to do to live a long, happy, healthy life. But here I was, crumpled on the stretcher, wondering how much life I actually had left.

I wondered how worthwhile overworking really was if I were to die tomorrow. I thought about how much effort I put into overtraining and maintaining appearances at the gym, and whether it was worth it if I might not see tomorrow. I reflected on all the times I hustled and stressed, pondering what would happen if I were to essentially die the next day. Oh, how I rushed through my life and how quickly my twenties slipped by. It was gone just like that because I was never truly present. How much of it was worth it? As I lost myself in thought, I heard a knock at the door.

It was my sister Angelique and her boyfriend Pete. They walked in, looked at me with a kind of sadness seeing me in a depressed state, trying their best to lift my spirits, while I felt like a burden to everyone else. I didn't want to take away from their fun and vacation because

I hadn't seen my sister and Pete for several years until this moment. They came to say their goodbyes before heading back to Thailand to focus on work and their clients. And here I was, basically wondering if I was going to live or not.

They asked me what was wrong, what they found out. I told them I ended up catching pneumonia, so there was a lot of liquid in my lungs. On top of that, they found a bubble in one of my lungs, which took up space, making it harder to breathe. That, combined with the liquid, didn't help. On top of that, they found out that my gut issue was probably not helping either. The GERD, the gastritis, the ulcers that ran havoc in my gut, Angelique and Pete looking at me with just pure sadness, I was still wondering, *how did I get here?*

I did everything right; I played everything by the book. I was healthy, but why did I feel so unwell? It didn't seem fair that I couldn't eat the foods I wanted, that I struggled to breathe, and that I had to worry the people around me. I remember laughing at my friend Chang when we lived together in Bali. He would always tell me, "Mike, go with the flow. You don't have to rush. You don't have to chase."

My younger, earlier twenties self that had something to prove said, "No, I don't have any time. I need to work. I need to hustle. I need to grind."

He said, "No, you need to relax."

I need to let go, I thought. *That's easy for you to say, but for me, it's hard to let go. I have so much family and financial responsibility. I can't just let go.*

Oh, how I wish I had listened to my friend Chang's wisdom I mocked earlier as lazy, because I didn't want to be seen that way.

Now I was regretting not taking his advice and not going with the flow in my work, my health, my eating habits, and my need to chase validation. And I was also caught up in needing approval from others while trying to be perfect as the good son, the good brother, the good provider, and the good protector. It felt heavy and exhausting. I thought I could hold onto it forever. But now, I was crumbling away. This was when I learned the most important concept of *Yǎng Shēng*.

Yǎng Shēng (yahng shung): The nourishing life. Because nature has its rhythms, and here I was disrespecting it. I would eat when I wanted to eat. I would train when I wanted to train. I didn't care about my sleep. I didn't care about relaxing. I didn't care about letting go. I tried banding it, Band-Aiding it with supplements, intense workouts, and biohacks. Yet, I still felt depleted. In that moment, I no longer questioned what my friend Chang told me when he taught me about *Yǎng Shēng*. Instead, it was blatantly obvious that *Yǎng Shēng* was the answer to the life that I was missing.

What Is *Yǎng Shēng*? Translation: '养 *(yǎng)*' means to nourish, raise, or cultivate. '生 *(shēng)*' means life, birth, or vitality. Together, *Yǎng Shēng* is not a treatment. It is a philosophy of living, one that nourishes life before sickness ever arrives. It is the art of gentle prevention, not reactive cure. In Chinese medicine, it is said, "Prevention is better than treatment. Nourishment is better than repair."

Where Western health culture often waits for the body to scream, *Yǎng Shēng* listens to the body when it whispers. In the Western biohacker mindset, the body is a machine to be hacked, optimized, and outsmarted. Sleep less. Work more. Pop a supplement. Compensate with caffeine. Grind harder. In *Yǎng Shēng*, the body is a garden. Not to be conquered, but to be cultivated gently.

"To live long, live slow." Ancient Chinese Proverb.

Yǎng Shēng aligns with the cycles of the earth: rise with the sun, rest with the moon, eat with the seasons, move with gentleness, feel with honesty. It neither punishes nor forces the body; instead, it honors it.

A young warrior once visited an old farmer in the hills of Yunnan, asking for the secret to strength and long life.

"Teach me how to become unbreakable," said the warrior.

The farmer handed him a bowl of warm millet and sat down under a peach tree.

"When I was your age," the farmer said, "I too thought strength was in the blade and muscle. But now I know strength is in knowing **when to plant, when to rest, and when to let go.** My greatest victory was not in war but in watching my children grow while I still had the strength to lift them."

The warrior wept, not because of weakness, but because no one had ever told him it was safe to slow down.

Today, we live in a modern health trap. It optimizes our pain rather than nourishing our vitality. Today, we count macros but ignore mealtimes, lift heavy but sleep late, buy adaptogens but skip rest. Drink protein shakes but forget to chew our food. Live in light but avoid the sun. We chase hacks, but *Yǎng Shēng* teaches harmony. It doesn't mean you stop working. It means you learn when to pause. You stop bullying your body and begin befriending it.

Practicing *Yǎng Shēng* is relatively simple. These are small, seasonal rhythms that are gentle but powerful. The goal is to nourish the body so that illness never takes hold. It is broken down by the seasons as follows.

In the spring → light greens, sprouts, liver cleansing foods

In the summer → cooling foods: melons, cucumber, mung bean tea

In the autumn → root vegetables, pears, white fungus (lung support)

In the winter → warming broths, black sesame, ginger, bone soups

In terms of time, it requires discipline.

➤ Wake early (between 5–7 a.m., lung Qi is strongest)

➤ Avoid late nights (liver detoxes between 1–3 a.m.)

➤ Light dinners, eaten before sunset

What the daily habits look like:

➤ Warm water upon waking

➤ Herbal teas based on constitution (goji berry, chrysanthemum, ginger)

➤ Walking after meals (especially evening digestion walks)

➤ Avoid raw, cold foods in excess

➤ Weekly space for emotional release: tears, prayer, or stillness

Emotions are an extremely important part of *Yǎng Shēng*. If they aren't released in the right way, they come out in more hidden paths.

For example, anger damages the liver, worry harms the spleen, and fear affects the kidneys. *Yǎng Shēng* teaches that health is not just physical but also emotional. Of course, we have work and careers where sometimes we can't control our external situations. Constant comparison doesn't help either. Western ambition urges you to grow like a skyscraper... fast, straight, tall. Chinese wisdom says: Grow like bamboo. For the first three years: invisible growth. Roots deepen. Then: rapid, graceful expansion. But always flexible. Never forced.

"The strongest trees are not the tallest. They are the ones that bend with the wind." Chinese proverb.

How the West Gets Health Wrong

Mainstream Health	*Yǎng Shēng*
Fitness at all costs.	Rest is sacred.
Supplements fix all.	Simplicity over excess.
Health is a six-pack.	Health is quiet energy.
Sleep is optional.	Sleep is medicinal.
Hustle = worth	Harmony = worth
Food is fuel.	Food is seasonal medicine.

When I finally left the hospital, I knew I needed a serious change. I began applying *Yǎng Shēng* principles to my life. I forgot everything I previously knew about health, and in the following days, I followed these rituals to cultivate *Yǎng Shēng*.

Morning

➤ Wake at 6 a.m. Drink warm water with lemon or ginger.

➤ Go outside and get sun for thirty minutes.

➤ Do five minutes of joint mobility or *qìgōng*.

➤ Eat breakfast within one hour of waking. Warm, light, nourishing.

Midday

➤ Main meal at 11 a.m.–1 p.m.

➤ Avoid cold drinks and processed food.

➤ Eat slowly. Chew twenty-plus times per bite.

Evening

➤ Light soup dinner before sunset.

➤ Walk for 10–20 minutes after dinner.

➤ No screens after 8 p.m.

➤ Sleep by 10 p.m. at the latest. No exceptions.

Emotional Care

➤ Journal: "Where am I forcing life?"

➤ Speak aloud to your body: "Thank you. I release the pressure."

➤ Practice five minutes of still breathing with hands on the belly.

I once believed health was something to conquer. That strength came from steel will and sleepless nights. But my body broke down, not because I was weak, but because I forgot that nature doesn't rush. The sun never hurries. The moon never skips its phase. Yet both accomplish everything. *Yǎng Shēng* is not a cure. It is a return. A return to slowness. A return to rhythm. A return to a way of life that nourishes not just your body, but your soul. If you're reading this now, exhausted, burnt out, anxious, maybe it's time to stop asking, "How can I heal faster?" and start asking, "How can I live slower?"

CHAPTER 3

Wú Wéi

(無為)

EFFORTLESS ACTION

―――∽m――――

I felt the warmth of the sun on my closed eyes. I already experienced the natural urge to dive into my daily responsibilities, but I allowed myself to just breathe for a minute or two before getting up. As I woke, I realized it was only 7 a.m., and I had been following the flow of what my friend Chang essentially told me. Instead of rushing into the day, tune into the rhythm of nature and avoid rushing; instead, slow things down.

See, this was very hard for me, and it really took me a lot of training to finally learn to relax, to tell my nervous system that I'm safe and that I don't have to worry all the time. I took a deep breath, allowed myself just one more minute in bed instead of rushing, which was something I wasn't used to.

I ended up going upstairs to my mom's condo, which, funny

enough, was only a couple of floors above mine. It's so funny, when I was younger, I wanted to run away from my mom and dad. I wanted to leave because of all the financial trauma we experienced, but as I got older and understood more about what life was really like, I ended up moving into a condo near my mom and dad, realizing they wouldn't be around forever.

I remember my friend asked me how many times I saw my mom and dad, and I told them only once a year. They said we needed to see each other more, and I was like, "What are you talking about?"

He said, "Well, how old's your dad?" I said he was seventy-two. "How old's your mom?" Fifty-eight. "Okay, well, if they only have, say, twenty more years, if you only see them once a year, you're only going to see them twenty more times before you never see them again."

When he said that, it hit me hard, but I didn't respond. Now that I was sick and spending more time with my mom and dad, I was so grateful that life almost took me away, only to bring me back home so I could spend more time with them as they aged. As I thought about this, I reached my mom's room. I opened the door and saw her already stressed and flustered. She still had that worried look on her face like moms do, but now she looked much older and more stressed out than she did when she held my small five-year-old body near that baseball park when I first learned about death. She was determined to do whatever it took to make sure I got better and returned to full strength.

Now, the thing about my mom is she wasn't able to get the hang of her Chinese philosophy of slowing down for health reasons, unlike my dad. I mean, my dad was seventy-two, could do twenty push-ups and pull-ups, and took 10,000 to 15,000 steps daily. My mom, however, faces more challenges with her health, blood, and genetics, making it much harder for her to lose the weight she's gained, especially after menopause. Still, she wanted her son to get stronger, so she decided to walk with me every day—slowly, steadily, without rushing—simply walking in nature together each morning before I started work.

I remember the first time we started walking, how difficult it was for me to keep up with her, how funny it was that I was supposed to be in my prime, yet I couldn't even keep up with my fifty-eight-year-old mom walking. I started to understand what she experienced when I was twelve. I would wait for her after school when she got home from work. She took me to the gym to play basketball while she did her weights, treadmill, and elliptical, always trying to get healthy. No matter what she did, she couldn't seem to lose weight.

She couldn't seem to maintain her weight whenever she did lose any. I believe it's also because of the stress she faced from double shifts as a nurse, arguments with my dad, and concerns about her kids growing up and receiving a good education. Her need for control and her desire to keep her family safe, which I really appreciate, eventually harmed her health. This made it very hard for her to regain a healthy weight. Something funny ended up happening. Every single day, we would walk with minimal effort. We woke up with the sun, walked, talked, and shared memories. We did this consistently for months.

After several months of doing that, I noticed something different. My mom started looking younger. The inflammation in her face began to decrease. She started losing weight. Her friends thought that she was on some magical drug or pill. They asked her, "What have you been doing?" She told them, "I've literally been just walking with my son every morning for an hour. We wake up with the sun. We walk. We talk. We laugh. And that's it."

This was when I truly understood what my friend Chang calls *Wú Wéi (woo way)*, which is often mistranslated in Taoism as doing nothing, non-force, non-striving, or effortless action. Just as water flows around rocks, nourishes without effort, and gradually erodes valleys, our actions should also stem from harmony rather than force. The balance point between extremes is what's called the *Dào*. The *Dào* represents the natural flow of the universe. Living in *Wú Wéi* means aligning yourself with the *Dào*.

"The highest virtue is like water. It benefits all and does not compete." Lao Tzu

I saw that with my mom's weight. With every diet she tried, the thing that actually helped her lose weight and keep it off was stopping the chasing and just walking with her son for an hour every single day in the morning. The natural flow of events was for her and me to simply walk every single day.

She accidentally discovered the best thing that is literally free for her to do to essentially melt off her weight and improve her skin, which hadn't looked this way in decades, through *Wú Wéi*, or non-action, by walking. Through alignment with the *Dào*. The *Dào* that initially seemed like a curse, with me in a hospital breathing through tubes for several days, was actually a blessing because it got my mom moving without force or grasping, but out of love for her son to get stronger. It makes me think about how *Wú Wéi* is a concept that most people don't take seriously because it appears lazy to those who don't understand it.

It's funny because I think about my GERD, gastritis, ulcers, and pneumonia. Many of which are just a physical manifestation of my need for control. My need for control stemmed from my lack of inner safety that was embedded in my nervous system as a child.

"Letting go" and not doing anything seemed like a completely different language that I couldn't understand. But I kept reflecting on the parables Chang would tell me when we were living together.

Chang used to tell me a story about a man trying to hold onto a butterfly. The harder he gripped, the more damage he did to its wings. But when he loosened his hands, the butterfly would rest there on its own. My soul was the butterfly, and my need for control was the tight grip on my life, trying to keep everything perfectly in place. My grip was so tight that it felt like my gut was being crushed.

The more I observe, the more I notice *Wú Wéi* in places where people live to be a hundred years old. These include Sardinia, Italy; Okinawa, Japan; and small islands in Greece. In the blue zones, elders don't schedule gym sessions; they walk to the market and tend their gardens, moving naturally with the rhythm of the day. Okinawan centenarians live with ease, purpose, and a sense of community. There's no rushing. The slowest aging people are often the calmest. Not because they do more, but because they resist less, which leads to less stress. Stress and cortisol destroy skin, digestion, and immune health. Flow heals.

Western wellness promotes, "Optimize harder." Routines are filled with cold plunges, supplements, wearables, and stress over self-care.

Wú Wéi says, "Let go of the unnatural striving." True vitality isn't effortful. It's what remains when resistance melts.

I learned that the lessons I apply to my life in health, career, relationships, friendships, and my surroundings can relate to the idea of *Wú Wéi*, which means doing less to achieve more. It is quite simple. When something outside my control comes and moves me into a new direction, I do the following: I breathe. I pause and reflect before moving. I replace urgency with rhythm. I respond, don't react. I let go of control, even for one breath, one hour, one walk. I choose inner quiet over outer noise, especially when making decisions.

For my health, it meant not chasing the latest fad, supplement, or craze, but modeling what the blue zones and the people who live there and live until one hundred naturally do to live a long, happy, and healthy life. That is to walk, to move with nature, to walk the stairs, to sit on the ground, to just keep moving. Not because you have to exercise, but because that's just the way you do it.

For example, now, instead of always taking a taxi, if the gym is only a couple of kilometers from my house, I'll just walk or ride a bicycle. When it comes to terms of my career and wealth, when my sickness got worse and I was going in and out of hospitals, I couldn't work as effectively as possible. And I was afraid because I felt that if I let go and didn't control my career, then I wouldn't be able to provide for my mom and dad, as they were financially dependent on me. And I was afraid of just letting go. I was afraid that my income would stop and dry up. I was afraid the bills would stack up. I was afraid of not feeling safe again. A lot of reminders from my youth.

When I had no other choice but to let go because I couldn't work while in the hospital, I had to learn to trust my colleagues and business partners and to let go of the responsibilities I was essentially clinging to for control. I clung to control because I was afraid of my worth. I felt that if I were to just let go, then my income would dry up. I felt like if I took my foot off the pedal, income would slow down because that's the story I learned in my childhood, watching my mom and dad work and sacrifice their lives for mine. But the more I let go and the more I gave responsibility to other people, and I allowed people to step into the responsibilities that I was controlling because it was tied to my identity, the more certain colleagues and business partners ended up taking those responsibilities off my plate, did a better job than I did, and were more fulfilled.

What surprised me most was that I ended up making more by doing less. By doing less in relationships, it got even easier. Around this period of time, I went through a very traumatic experience where I was trying to start a family, and I was trying to force it to happen as fast as possible. However, the natural flow of life pushed my partner and me in two opposite directions at that time. I was striving to control it, to keep the butterfly in place that was the relationship that I had. Eventually, I had to learn how to breathe, to pause, to not react to the trauma that I experienced of us being torn away from each other, and my heart left in broken pieces. The more I accepted that heartbreak was meant for me and not against me, the more I was able to go with the flow of life. I stopped reacting and trying to control the reality I desired.

What I didn't expect was that the heartbreak healed on its own. Then I bumped into somebody who was more aligned with my values of how I actually want to raise my future kids. It is the same with friendships. You know, before, I was very insecure around friends because I thought that they didn't want to hang out with me. And then, when I started building businesses, I was surrounded by people who only wanted certain things, not an authentic friendship.

When I lost a lot of money as the business went downhill, even though I initially let go of the responsibilities, I lost a lot of friends. The ones that ended up staying, I realized, were actually the deeper friendships and relationships I needed to spend more time in, going deeper rather than wider with a bunch of random people.

The more I allowed *Wú Wéi* to work, the more life just started happening, and I cannot explain it. What I've learned from *Wú Wéi* is that you need patience. Because sometimes life looks worse before it looks better. For example, my health, I'm just not feeling well. Now, I'm just walking every single day. Maybe some push-ups here, maybe some pull-ups there. My friends are making fun of me because of how unhealthy I look, just walking, doing pull-ups and push-ups. I feel anxious trying to keep up with others, and I want to rush back to the gym, do the fat-burning exercises, and take excessive amounts of supplements. But I have to catch myself because I know that that's not the game I'm playing. I'm playing the game so I can pick up my great-grandkids, throw them up in the air, and catch them when I'm in my nineties. Not the game where I focus on health so much and end up getting a hip or knee injury, which would lead to a lower quality of life in my middle years. It's also the exact same thing in careers or businesses.

When you let go, things will crash before they get better. Trusting in the natural flow of life, you can choose to observe instead of react. This allows you to see events like waves. Some of these waves can help you. Instead of struggling to reach your goals, you can ride these waves and move toward what you want with less effort. This means following the natural rhythm of the universe as it guides you in the right direction.

When I fully accepted *Wú Wéi*, after the trial period that tested my patience, all aspects of my life improved. My health got better. My relationships got better. My wealth got better. Through my sickness, which I thought was a curse, I moved closer to my mom and dad, which then got my mom to start losing weight. During those months, my mom lost over twenty pounds by walking every single day. Now, if you had asked me if my sickness was a blessing when I was in the hospital, I would have told you no. But if you ask me now, I'd say yes, because it brought me closer to my mom and dad. It got my mom to lose weight. It got my dad to look even younger.

Here are some of the biggest things to cultivate the power of *Wú Wéi* when the world seems too chaotic to control:

- ➤ Morning tea ritual in silence before checking messages.
- ➤ Walking without a podcast, letting thoughts settle like stirred water.
- ➤ Saying "no" without guilt.
- ➤ Scheduling space between meetings or obligations.
- ➤ Letting ideas ripen before forcing action.
- ➤ Sit quietly by water or a window each day, doing nothing.
- ➤ Schedule one "margin hour" daily, a time with no task.
- ➤ Remove one obligation a week that no longer serves you.
- ➤ Replace one reaction with a pause.
- ➤ Let yourself feel: "I don't need to force today. What wants to happen?"

The *Dào* does not arrive loudly. It enters like a breeze through an open window. It needs no forcing, no fixing. Only space to flow. Youth is not stored in your effort; it is revealed in your ease. When you stop gripping so tightly, you find what was always trying to hold you.

CHAPTER 4

Zhōng Yōng

(中庸)

THE GOLDEN MEAN

~~

Fast forward several years after the emergency room incident, and I had built my strength back up. I was back at my sister's house in Thailand with her boyfriend, my mom, and my dad as we prepared for my sister's twenty-eighth birthday. I had an ulterior motive for this visit. My mother had lost twenty pounds; my father looked more vibrant and younger. My sister worked in balance. Every single person in my family was in harmony with the *Dào*. Everyone but me.

You see, my personality is very interesting because I tend to always swing between different extremes. For example, I'll be vegan and then I'll be a carnivore. I'll eat a lot of calories, or I'll focus on fasting. I'm a workaholic, or I'll explode from all the stress and just not do any work. My life has always been from one extreme to another extreme. Obviously, it's not good, especially with my health. It seemed like, as healthy as I got in the several years after that emergency room incident, I was starting to move to the opposite extreme once again.

I noticed that whenever I started becoming constipated, my bowel movements were a physical manifestation of my internal insecurities and my need to control. With stresses at work and in business, I noticed that I was starting to swing to the other extreme with work, whereby my health would eventually suffer.

Luckily, I knew this. So, I ended up forcing myself to surround myself with people who lived in harmony with the *Dào*. I essentially had to check into my sister's home because my overambition was causing me to start relapsing back toward an extreme that I knew was not good for me. The need to prove to others that I'm successful, the need to chase validation, the need to try to prove to people that I'm smart or good, all the masks I wear from the insecurities of my childhood. While I was in my sister's kitchen, I thought it was a good idea to eat three pounds of purple sweet potatoes. I read in a book about longevity that many centenarians in Japan mainly eat purple sweet potatoes. My sister Angelique looked at me and said, "Mike, you're kind of extreme."

I looked at her almost like a rabid animal. "What do you mean?" I asked as purple crumbs of sweet potato seemed to fall out of my big bowl and onto the floor, where her cute little white cat tried licking them for a taste.

My sister said, "Well, you really go from one end to another. It seems like it doesn't work. So why don't you just eat what we eat and do what we do?"

Little did I know that I had just signed up for an overambitious intervention in which my life was to go back and find my center by modeling how my dad, my mom, my sister, and Pete lived in their *Dào*.

Now, what this really means is a Chinese concept called *Zhōng Yōng (jong yong)*, which I learned from my friend Chang when we lived together. He often told me that *Zhōng Yōng* means "center and constant," usually seen as the doctrine of the mean or the golden path. It's a key Confucian idea that basically says virtue isn't found in excess but in moderation. Not mediocrity, but deliberate balance.

Confucius, who lived over 2,500 years ago, was a Chinese philosopher and teacher whose ideas shaped much of East Asian culture and moral thought. He believed that harmony within oneself, one's family, and society was the foundation of a good life. To him, true virtue was never found in extremes, whether indulgence or deprivation, but in balance. Mastery of life meant staying centered in the storm. The greatest wisdom, he taught, was not in chasing perfection but in maintaining harmony with others and with the natural rhythms of the world.

When I first heard these teachings, they sounded poetic but abstract. It wasn't until I started applying them to my own life that I realized how practical they truly were. *Zhōng Yōng* wasn't just philosophy; it was a daily practice. It shaped how I ate, how I worked, and how I learned to find balance again after years of swinging between extremes.

Zhōng Yōng is the heartbeat of sustainable vitality. It is the middle path. When we swing between obsession and avoidance, we become unstable. Balance creates resilience, like a tree rooted in flexible soil. In Chinese medicine, health is harmony between *yin* and *yang*; excess in either direction becomes illness. Even the excess of a good thing can become an imbalance.

I think about how I used to think before I developed all my gut issues. I can see old me mocking the idea of *Zhōng Yōng*. But now I see the wisdom in plain sight. Let's take, for example, water. Consuming too much water in a short period can be fatal. Let's take vegetables. I was so afraid of my constipation coming once again that I would eat bowls and bowls of broccoli and spinach to prevent it from happening. Guess what that ended up doing? Making me even more constipated. I heard olive oil was the secret to longevity, so I just started pouring it on every single one of my meals. Made the gut issues worse. I heard oysters were good for male vitality from some health guru. I found a local fisherman back when I was living in Bali, and he would give me fresh oysters daily for a low price. I ended up getting severe mercury poisoning like an idiot.

Too much of anything good becomes bad. But also in the same light, too much of anything bad can also become good. An example was my gut issues and health. That "bad" was what pushed me closer to my family and got my mom and dad to really start taking these ancient Chinese secrets even more seriously, since we had to do them together.

This is the *yin* and the *yang*. The push and the pull. The up and the down, the good and the bad.

My friend Chang would tell me sometimes about a parable his grandfather would tell him.

A man once sought to live forever, so he only drank herbal tonics and fasted for weeks. His body thinned, his eyes sharpened like blades, and he believed he had mastered life. One day, an old farmer passed him and laughed: "You have eaten wind and called it wisdom. But the tree lives long because it drinks both sun and rain." The man realized then, longevity is not purity. It is rhythm.

Zhōng Yōng naturally appears in many areas today. It appears in the blue zones where people don't count macros; they just eat until 80% full. They walk, garden, rest, and repeat. The Okinawans say "*hara hachi bu*," which means stop eating when you're no longer hungry, not when you're stuffed. This is probably my biggest struggle so far. It shows up in stress management, too. High performers often crash because they only know two gears: full throttle or complete shutdown.

I'm guilty of that, as you can see from my crazy extremes' intervention at my sister's birthday. As I spent more time with my family, who naturally lived in the *Dào*, I slowly started finding my center once again, as my bowel movements returned to consistency by just monkey-seeing-monkey-doing the people around me who were in rhythm. I used to think "more was more." More gym, more hustle, more caffeine. But now I think: less, done daily, creates more over time.

Here are the beliefs that I had to shatter to prevent myself from going to an extreme that inevitably destroys my health.

Mainstream Extremes vs. Confucian Balance

Modern Culture	*Zhōng Yōng* Philosophy
Fasting for seventy-two hours	Eating until 80% full
Biohacking with fifteen pills	Eating fresh, local, simple
Hustle till burnout	Work with rest woven in

All-or-nothing mindset	Gradual, rhythmic consistency
Emotional outbursts	Daily self-regulation practices

Mainstream worships extremes because they're louder, sexier, and easier to market. *Zhōng Yōng* whispers, "Choose the middle, not because it's safe, but because it's strong."

To apply *Zhōng Yōng*, consider replacing "intensity" with rhythm. Embracing a steady and balanced approach can create a more sustainable path to success. Additionally, replace "optimization" with presence. Focusing on being fully engaged in the moment allows for deeper connections and a more meaningful experience. Finally, instead of relying on "ten-step hacks," focus on one thing done daily. Consistent, small actions can lead to significant progress over time.

For the next ten days, I lived with my sister in her spare bedroom. I shared my bed with her cute little cat, who would wake me up each morning by brushing against my leg. This was part of the routine she set for me:

➢ Mindful Portions – Eat slowly, chew fully, stop before full.

➢ Work-Rest Rhythm – Use natural light to cue work/wind-down.

➢ Emotional Check-ins – Midday breathwork, journaling, stillness.

➢ Daily Walking – Not for exercise, but for regulation.

➢ Sleep at Consistent Times – Respecting your circadian rhythm.

➢ Relational Moderation – Neither cling nor withdraw. Stay

steady.

➤ Minimal Stimulants – Enjoy tea or coffee with intention, not addiction.

➤ Digital Boundaries – Don't scroll after sundown. Let dopamine rest.

Here are the next action steps she had me follow:

➤ Eat until 80% full this week. No macros. Just presence.

➤ Cancel one thing from your calendar that you added out of ego.

➤ Schedule one "middle moment" per day. A walk, a nap, a tea break.

➤ Reflect: where am I chasing "more" out of fear instead of need?

➤ Speak to yourself kindly. Harsh inner voices are another form of excess.

I had to learn to be okay with the "middle." I had to relearn how to get used to being centered instead of living in extremes. Because what I failed to realize is that between fire and ice, there is warmth. Between starving and stuffing, there is satisfaction. Between ambition and apathy, there is purpose. The middle is not mediocrity. It is where your soul has space to breathe. *Zhōng Yōng* is not a compromise. It is a crown worn quietly. Let the world chase more. You choose enough.

CHAPTER 5

Five Elements

(五行)

LIVING IN RHYTHM WITH NATURE

———*m*———

I was waiting in a clinic in Bali for my blood test results. I felt calm and relaxed because I knew I was young and healthy. I only took the tests because my friend did and said it was good to check. Like many people interested in health, I decided to get tested. While I sat in the waiting room, I looked at the supplements on the counter, the dusty books on the shelf, and the receptionist, who seemed focused on a book, waiting for someone to walk through the door.

"Michael, the doctor's ready with your results. You may now enter the room."

I walked in to see the doctor once again. She was a German lady. She ended up building a practice in Bali focused on health and wellness, employing a holistic approach. She had me take a seat right next to this long stretcher that she used to adjust patients and give them checkups. I sat there, confident, knowing that I probably had nothing wrong with me. As she showed me the results of my blood test, she said there was something very odd about the way my blood pellets clumped. I was a little bit concerned. So, like any other person who was addicted to the biohacking realm, I started getting more blood tests. I gave hair samples. I gave them poop samples just to test what was going on. After what seemed like several weeks to get the results back after the lab analyzed it, it turned out that what I had was extreme mercury poisoning.

When they gave me the charts, they said the mercury level in my blood was essentially off the charts. I heard about mercury poisoning before. It's what happens when a significant amount of toxins accumulates in your body. It could be from the water source that you drink. It could be from a certain type of seafood you might eat. I started wondering, *where could this have possibly come from? Could it be from all the oysters I ate for what I thought would improve my male vitality?*

I thought, *Oh, if oysters are so good, I might as well just have them every day.* For a year, I ate raw oysters every single day, simply because the guru said they were good for me. A year later, I had enough mercury poisoning that it was startling. If I didn't do something about it long-term, then I could end up with permanent damage to my brain and spinal cord or even die. This was when I learned the concept that too much of a good thing can be a bad thing, and how I really needed to embrace living in rhythm with nature.

You see, nature didn't always give you an abundance of oysters back in the ancient days. Sometimes, you have oysters; sometimes, you don't. Sometimes, you have fish; sometimes, you don't. The way that nature moves is that it gives you variety so that you're not too extreme on one specific ingredient. I learned about the concept of the five elements, which involves living in harmony with nature and aligning ourselves with its rhythms: wood, fire, earth, metal, and water. This understanding helps us connect with the cycles of life, energy, and the seasons. It also highlights the importance of focusing on specific organs in our bodies and choosing foods that contribute to our youthfulness. When I began to realize this, I became intrigued. Not only intrigued, I knew I needed to find an answer or else this mercury poisoning could mess up my mind, my body, my longevity, my life.

The doctor instructed me to follow a protocol to remove the mercury, but she shared some additional information with me before I left. "Mike, you do know this protocol will just remove the mercury from your system, but if you don't find a way to remove the source of the mercury, it will easily come back."

So many times, I wanted a "protocol" to fix my pain. I never thought about removing the source that caused the pain. It reminds me of when I was younger and I was dating a narcissist. I was wondering why I was feeling so much anxiety and couldn't sleep. It also didn't help that I was a severe chronic people-pleaser. I tried every hack to relax my nervous system, but I never stopped dating that narcissist. When we broke up, for some reason, all my ailments just disappeared. I realized that for me, the culprit for my gut was primarily the lifestyle choices I made out of habit, just so I didn't have to think. The water I drink, the restaurants I eat in, the stress from work, traffic, and responsibilities. So much of my nervous system was tied to my environment. So, like any crazy person would do, I wanted to test the opposite.

So, during this period, I wanted to live on a farm. I wanted to experience what it was like to really be with nature and how different it was from mainstream thinking. So, I found a farm where I could live. It was very interesting going there. It was far from my ancestral home in the Philippines, in a little village with no internet whatsoever. So already I felt the anxiety come up, what about my work? What about the messages that I had to answer? I needed to heal my body, and I needed to do it with nature that has existed for thousands of years, not some latest hack that someone is going to tell me is the truth. When I arrived at the farm, the family was quite confused. They were unsure about this random guy moving in with them for a week. My purpose was to experience their daily life, eat what they typically ate, and assist them on the farm.

My first experience was when I walked in, and the mom and dad looked at me, sizing me up, wondering who I was. My friend who recommended this farm introduced me to the person whose parents lived there. As my guide interpreted what I wanted to say to the parents, the parents laughed and smiled and told me, "Okay." After which the mom went over to the chicken coop, grabbed a chicken that looked oh-so-cute, and looked into its eyes. It was the first time that I could actually understand her, because I couldn't understand the dialect she used. She literally looked at me and said, "Prepare dinner."

Now, as I was holding this live chicken in my hand, I wasn't sure if I was doing the right thing or the wrong thing. She went to the corner and taught me to respect the chicken before preparing it, especially before beheading it, just like they did in ancient and medieval times. It was then that I regretted my decision to live on the farm.

She motioned with her hand as she brought me over to the side of the hut. She got deep in a squat where her butt touched the ground, which is what a lot of Asian cultures do to eat, hang out, talk, and wait. She effortlessly, in her late fifties, got to the deepest squat that I'd ever seen with ease. Then she showed me where to actually slice it in the neck so it's quick for the chicken and painless. She handed me the knife. I felt butterflies in my stomach, guilt rising because I'd never done this before. I wanted to cry because the chicken looked so cute. As she gave me the knife, which seemed a little dull, I tried to do it in one go, like a swift samurai, but I couldn't.

The chicken, with the neck so strong, kept on looking at me, almost like pleading with its eyes to hurry up. But no matter how hard I tried with the knife, it just wouldn't go through. The chicken, looking at me, looking very impatient, now looked over to the mom. She just grabbed the chicken from my hand and the knife. With one sweep of the knife, she cleanly beheaded the chicken. I was disappointed in myself and my inability to finish it, but she gave me the chicken and said, "Okay, you pluck the feathers."

What we had to do was put it in boiling water to soften the feathers, so it would be easy to pull out. I plucked each one of the feathers as I sat there in my tent in a deep squat, knowing my Asian ancestors would be disappointed in how bad my hips and knees were. I started thinking about how interesting it was to live in nature. How literally nature will bring things into your life and take things away.

The natural abundance of certain ingredients and the scarcity of others are actually nature's way of ensuring you're in rhythm with your health and longevity. Making sure your organs get the right nutrients when they need them, at the right time of year. And to make sure you are in sync, which made me realize maybe the secret isn't more effort, but more alignment.

For the next several days, I was in awe because, as my anxiety about the world and city life started calming down, I began to see a sense of stillness on this farm and how time moved differently there. When I was in the modern world, I was burnt out, my digestion was off, my skin felt dull, no matter how many superfoods I tried or supplements, protocols, or diets. Then I noticed how the people of this village lived; they were aligned with the seasons. They drank warm soup whenever it was cold. They rose early with the sun. They sweated out toxins in the summer heat. They didn't know the science, but they were in sync.

The sixty-year-olds, seventy-year-olds, and eighty-year-olds were far healthier than I've ever seen anywhere else in the world. Many can still sit up from the floor, do manual labor in the fields, and even outdrink any one of my old college friends with their natural coconut wine, which they make. My realization and reflection were that I was longing to feel in flow like them. All of the things that they were doing were things that anybody can do. Their workouts were just planting, gardening, or sitting in a deep squat when they hung out. They sometimes sat on the floor when they were eating, so they naturally moved from low to high, and they never had hip or knee problems. They aged gracefully because they spent their time not in front of screens, but laughing together.

Even when they poop, the way their toilets are set up, they're essentially connected to the ground in the village. So, instead of sitting on a porcelain throne, they end up squatting. I remember when the guide who essentially became my friend was like, "This is where we poop." And I'm like, "Really? It's just a hole in the ground. Where do you sit?" My friend looked at me.

"You don't; you hover."

"Hover?" I responded, confused.

"Yeah, you just hover."

I recall the first time I tried the concept of hovering to relieve myself; it was quite weird. It seems that the way we poop is not natural. When we sit, the alignment of our intestines and the area that releases the stool does not provide the best mechanics for fully relieving ourselves. When you squat, it's literally the perfect path for the poop to come out with the least amount of pressure to your gut as possible.

I remember how, when the day was super hot, they would stay inside and take a nap. They would then do a few light chores in the afternoon. Then they would prepare for dinner as the sun was setting. They would eat together either at the table or in a squatting position on the floor. I remember it was late, so we went to bed early, like 9 p.m., and then we woke up when we heard the roosters crow, which was around 5:30 or 6 a.m. We would work on the farm when it was not as hot, after eating a small meal. Then we would repeat.

For seven days, that's what I did. They were all experts at living long, happy, and healthy without all the "chasing" energy of the newest, latest health trend. For me, it felt weird getting into a deep Asian squat, even being Asian myself. It felt weird trying to poop while "hovering." It felt weird sleeping earlier and then waking up earlier. It felt strange not to have the same foods every day. One day, I would eat squash. The next day, I would have okra, a Filipino vegetable that feels slimy like spinach but tastes good. Another day, I would have bitter melon. On another day, I would try dragon fruit. It seemed like every day was something new, even though I was used to eating the same boring meals every single day. Within literally a couple of days, my constipation, which was usually chronic, was gone, as I was hovering like a pro.

I stopped eating the extreme foods I thought were the answer and focused on the balance of nature. I sweated out the toxins, meaning I didn't even really need to go in the sauna. I was one with nature. As I spent more time with that, I realized how I could integrate this back at home, because I couldn't live on the farm forever. It was a practice that I wanted to bring back. I began to realize that I needed to be very considerate of what nature was trying to tell me. What were my emotions trying to tell me? Because certain emotions and certain weathers in nature mean it's time for me to eat different things.

In terms of the five-element system, one of the oldest foundational principles of Chinese health, rooted in Taoism and Traditional Chinese Medicine, there are five elements that map to different seasons, organs, emotions, and tastes. Now these aren't just poetic metaphors; they are life's feedback loop, showing your body, your mind, and the external world are one ecosystem.

Spring – Wood – Liver – Sour – Anger

Summer – Fire – Heart – Bitter – Joy

Late Summer – Earth – Spleen – Sweet – Worry

Autumn – Metal – Lungs – Pungent – Grief

Winter – Water – Kidneys – Salty – Fear

The Taoists believe that we are not separate from nature. Health comes from living in harmony with its flows, not conquering them. The elements symbolize cycles of birth, growth, harvest, decay, and stillness, which exist within us. It's a radical concept in which youthfulness is not maintained by resisting aging, but by moving in sync with the natural seasons of our body and environment.

It reminds me of another parable Chang would tell me.

"Mike, one day, a young man builds a perfect greenhouse and forces his plants to grow faster with artificial light and constant watering. At first, they bloom wildly. But soon, they weaken, the soil turns sour, and the fruit loses flavor. His elder visits and simply opens the roof, letting the sun and wind in. Let them breathe. Let them rest when the earth rests. Let them grow when the season says grow."

I didn't realize this at the time, but I was using artificial light and constant watering, when what my mind, body, and spirit desperately needed was sun and wind. The message? Control is not harmony. Forcing nature breaks the rhythm that sustains life.

How this parable translates into modern culture is that burnout results from too much "fire." Every single day, we are overstimulated, addicted to caffeine, constantly comparing ourselves to others, and chasing joy instead of gratitude and contentment. With my bloating and gut issues, it meant I had a weak spleen from eating cold or sweet foods in the wrong season. With my anxiety and overthinking, it meant that my liver was experiencing stagnation due to a lack of movement and a need to detox. For my premature aging, it meant that I had a weak kidney from my lack of rest, my fear, and my overstimulation.

Western wellness often sees health as mechanical: fix this

hormone, track this macro, cut this food group. The five elements view health as relational and seasonal. You don't just eat what's healthy, you eat what your organ system needs in that season of the year and that phase of your life. Western view: Optimize. Eastern view: Harmonize.

Here's how the five-element system works with the seasons:

Spring – Wood – Liver – Sour – Anger

➤ Eat greens, sour foods (lemon, vinegar)

➤ Move your body to help energy flow

➤ Avoid bottling up emotion; express honestly

Summer – Fire – Heart – Bitter – Joy

➤ Lighter meals, bitter greens (ampalaya, dandelion)

➤ Social joy, but not overstimulation

➤ Sleep later, rise early, and embrace the sun

Late Summer – Earth – Spleen – Sweet – Worry

➤ Earthy foods: squash, root vegetables

➤ Slow chewing, no overeating

➤ Declutter your thoughts and environment

Autumn – Metal – Lungs – Pungent – Grief

➤ Eat radish, pears, and garlic

➤ Practice breathing, letting go

➤ Journal grief; don't suppress it

Winter – Water – Kidneys – Salty – Fear

➤ Warm foods: congee, soups, and seaweed

➤ Deep rest, stillness, and reflection

➤ Embrace inner fears gently, not escape

Each season has a distinct theme of food, a specific habit, and a particular emotional focus. All of it is connected. Your feelings are important and connected to the rhythm of the seasons. Having each of these seasons help you get your emotions in rhythm with the foods you eat and the habits you focus on is one of the best ways to feel more energy and vitality.

Now, here are essential Habits for Harmonizing with the Five Elements:

➤ Begin your day with a seasonal tea or broth.

➤ Rotate foods seasonally: bitter in summer, warming in winter.

➤ Practice seasonal movement: sweat in summer, stillness in winter.

➤ Perform seasonal "emotional check-ins" (What emotion is asking for expression?).

➤ Let your environment teach you what your body needs, not trends.

For example, one day after going through a crazy period of chronic constipation, I was worried about what I could do to fix it. The stress and overthinking made my constipation worse. While I was walking from the homestead where I was staying to the gym, I noticed this Filipino man climbing a tree. Curious, I asked what he was doing. He told me, "I get coconut."

That's when it hit me! Nature was giving me the answer all along. I was too busy focusing on trying to hack the poop. I asked for a coconut, he climbed up and chopped one down, and I drank it with joy. I was relieved shortly after. Spending time in nature provides you with everything you need to become healthier.

Remember this: You are not a machine that needs to be optimized. You are like a season in motion, a garden that holds memories, and a tide that knows when to rise and when to rest. When you stop pushing too hard, the youth you thought you lost can come back. This happens not because you try harder, but because you remember the natural rhythm of life. Live like a season, age gently, and heal like a flowing river.

CHAPTER 6

Shòu

(壽)

LONGEVITY AS A VIRTUE

~~~

M om, can you pass the rice?" I motioned over to my mom as we were sitting there at a dinner table in some random surf town in the Philippines. As my mom gave me the bowl of rice for my chicken soup, I noticed my dad quietly handing money to the guitarist who was playing at the outdoor restaurant where we were eating.

The month was April, and it was one of our family's quarterly ten-day travel stints together, allowing us to really bond as a family. My mom, dad, sister, and cousins even came along. While we were living in the surf town, we rented a room with nine beds, all in one room, smushed together. So, we all slept like sardines, just like we did back when I was younger.

Many of the things I crave now, as an adult, are the beautiful memories of simplicity from when I was younger. When we were younger, we were forced into closeness due to financial constraints, so we always shared beds and small rooms with a bunch of relatives. Now that we are older, many of my family members don't mind sleeping in the same room on the floor, with the beds pressed together.

Now we were at the restaurant, and my dad bribed the guitarist for some reason. I'd already seen this one too many times, so I knew what was coming, and I think my sister, cousins, and mom did, too. Right as I was putting the second spoon of rice into my mouth, I heard a noise from the speaker coming from the guitarist. "And, guys, I want to introduce you to a musician who came all the way from the Midwest of America to sing a song for you today. Welcome, Al!"

Al, the name given to my father at birth, the name of the man I didn't know could be happy or smile. Because when I was younger, he was always stressed. He always had a deep stress line in the middle of his eyebrows. His hair was graying. When I was younger, and I would talk out of turn, he would hit me or flick my ear as punishment. I was afraid of my dad. I was angry with him for being so strict. He often drank to escape problems and avoided fights with my mom. He gave up his dreams of starting a business to provide a stable life for us kids. He was quiet and reserved, only showing his anger. I never saw his fun side because he had so much stress from his responsibilities. Over the years, he gained weight and developed a beer belly in his fifties because of drinking. But now, I saw him walking across the restaurant with a big, cheerful smile.

No more beer belly, radiating with joy, face clean with very few wrinkles, a man who has recently just started vlogging and recording his travel vlogs. This man, who literally started creating videos on *tai chi* and now wears old kung-fu martial arts costumes around the house while looking like he's doing the Shaolin moves, where he wrestles with a fish with his hands. The man is passionately grabbing the microphone while the guitar plays, singing classic '70s rock music at the top of his lungs. He smiles and laughs, showcasing an incredible stage presence and confidence. Everyone in the dining room of this random restaurant is smiling, laughing, and clapping. My sister buries her face in her hands, a bit embarrassed but happy, while my mom rolls her eyes, thinking, "Here we go again." My cousins just look at my dad and laugh. It's actually a beautiful moment.

My dad didn't have this energy when I was younger. He was always stressed. I think something happened when he got older, especially when he no longer had to worry about the stress of providing for the family, because I then took up that role. As he got older, I noticed something beautiful, and that is the older your parents get, the more they revert to their childlike selves. If you would just allow it, the closer you get, you literally see your dad become a little boy again, and your mom become a little girl again. Here, I saw my dad, the man I feared greatly, turn into a little boy who was just playful, happy, kind, generous, worry-free, and happy-go-lucky. The man who became my best friend as I got older.

I love my dad so much. He's an example of what it means not to live a long life, but to really increase the quality of it as you get older. He's the man who, every single year, would call his friends, even if they were on the other side of the world, and say happy birthday at midnight. He's the man who taught me how to deal with rejection when I was younger because he would take my sister and me door-to-door, knocking on doors to leave calling cards for his heating-and-cooling side hustle, which involved air conditioning units. He's the same man who was now grabbing this microphone and singing.

One of my favorite things to do with my dad is to take spontaneous trips together, just the two of us. Sometimes, we go back to a surf island and live in a teepee while he films his *tai chi* videos in the ocean wearing his martial arts costume. We usually do this once or twice a year, our version of a boys' trip.

One October, we flew to a small island in the Philippines and became close to a local family. The moment we arrived, I rented a cheap motorbike, and my dad hopped on the back while gripping a selfie stick to film a vlog. It's always a funny sight to see him holding on tight as we ride through narrow roads toward the quieter parts of the island, far from any tourists.

That's how we met my surf instructor, a local who invited us into his home. It was built entirely from materials found on the island, like wood, bamboo, and palm leaves. He showed us the small garden in the back where his family grew most of their food. For lunch and dinner, we would eat with them, enjoying meals made from whatever they harvested or caught in the sea that day. My dad would sometimes pick up the old guitar lying in the corner and start singing, and soon, everyone would join in.

At night, we'd ride the motorbike back to our teepee, just a few minutes away. One morning, I woke up and couldn't find my dad anywhere. I walked toward the beach and saw him there, dressed in his martial arts outfit, slowly practicing *tai chi* against the rising sun. I couldn't help but laugh. Moments like that, quiet, strange, and beautiful, always stay with me.

He's also an outstanding networker. I didn't realize how charismatic he was until after he quit drinking, when I saw how much joy and harmony he embodies, surrounded by loyal friends. Whenever his friends are ill, he walks with them and shares his latest longevity tips, which he learned from either my friend Chang or the *tai chi* and *qìgōng* masters. At seventy-two, he is still chasing his dreams. He explores ways to build businesses not out of obligation, but simply because it brings him joy. For him, this pursuit keeps his mind young and connects him to his childhood passion. I've heard stories about my dad, stories I never believed.

When he was younger, he would sell random things on the streets in the Philippines, showing that he was always an entrepreneur. The stress of living in America really took away from his entrepreneurial spirit, but now he is filled with so much boyish energy once again.

My dad is a perfect example of what it means to live in *Shòu (show)*, which means longevity or long life. Now, in ancient China, *Shòu*, longevity as a virtue, was more than just living long. It was living wisely, peacefully, and in rhythm with the universe. *Shòu* is not just about lifespan, but the quality of your days. It's meant to live with dignity, harmony, joy, and contribution, and to cultivate habits that gently slow aging through breath, simplicity, and avoiding inner extremes.

My dad always says, "It's not about the years in your life, but the life in your years." Seeing my dad sing on stage while acting like a rock star in his twenties made me think: *what if being youthful isn't something we need to chase, but something we earn by living well?*

You see, *Shòu* was one of the five blessings in ancient Chinese culture. Those five blessings were longevity, wealth, health, virtue, and a peaceful death. But longevity came first, not for vanity, but because it represented a life lived in harmony. In Taoist and Confucian philosophy, a long life wasn't the goal. It was the result of moral alignment, right living, balanced thought, and attunement with nature. The long-lived man was gentle, slow to anger, content, and ate simply. *Shòu* is not a hack. It is a consequence of peaceful living. My dad is a perfect example of how someone could still live in *Shòu* after decades of stress, worry, anxiety from work, bills, and pain. My dad is a symbol that anyone, at any age, can start chasing their dreams, no matter how late it is. Whenever I travel with my dad, he's a perfect reminder of what *Shòu* is.

I remember we were driving around Surigao Island, trying to find farmland, because our family is addicted to *kamote (kah-MOH-teh)*, a type of Filipino sweet potato that tastes like cookies and cream when boiled and chilled overnight in the refrigerator. And just seeing my dad get on the back of my moped and hold me so tight as he took a selfie with his little camera, recording himself, filming a video, vlogging his adventures, I couldn't help but smile at the realization that this man was seventy-two years old. How much joy this man had. When I meet business partners, my dad is actually a secret weapon that de-armors very stiff people and helps soften them back to their inner child. My dad is a reminder that living a long life is a reward, not a right.

In the East, longevity is earned through one's character, who you are. In the West, it is pursued through control, which I learned the hard way. The big idea for me was that you do not age more slowly by force, but by becoming less reactive, less toxic, less hurried. The long-lived man is not obsessed with lifespan. He simply lives in a way that invites it, which is my father. He reminds me of a classic Taoist line that Chang would always say to me, "Mike, to lengthen your life, first lengthen your breath." My dad is the epitome of what it means to allow your breath to lengthen.

A parable that comes to mind is the parable of the two gardeners. One pruned his trees obsessively, measured each stem, used imported chemicals, and strange lights. His garden looked perfect for the season. Then it withered. The other watered his plants gently, let the wind shape them, and followed the lunar calendar. His fruits took longer to grow, but each season, they came back stronger, richer, and fuller. When asked the secret, he said, "I don't force life. I just let it live."

Now, where *Shòu* shows up in modern wellness and longevity is that modern blue zones accidentally confirm what ancient *Shòu* teaches. That is to eat with others. Being part of a community means lower stress and a longer life. Move naturally, not in extremes. Prioritize joy, faith, and meaningful work. Nap, walk, and rise with the sun. In both Okinawa and rural China, longevity is a lifestyle of soft edges, not a pursuit of performance.

How the West Gets Longevity Wrong

Western Longevity:	*Shòu* (壽) Longevity:
Biohack everything	Trust in rhythm
Extreme diets	Gentle, consistent meals
Obsession with lifespan	Focus on peace of mind
Stressful optimization	Relaxed daily rituals

Anti-aging creams	Pro-aging presence

Over-effort to live longer creates internal pressure, the very oxidative stress and inflammation we're trying to avoid. The *Shòu* way: Live clean, live light, live long.

How to Apply *Shòu* in Daily Life:

➤ Food: Eat mostly plant-based, warm meals. Chew slowly. Never overeat.

➤ Emotion: Avoid resentment and gossip. They age the heart.

➤ Sleep: Respect the sun. Go to bed early, rise without an alarm.

➤ Movement: Walk after every meal. Bend, stretch, breathe.

➤ Spirit: Cultivate peace. Unresolved anger is premature death.

➤ Joy: Laugh often, love long, and surround yourself with the young at heart.

Essential Habits for the Virtue of Long Life:

➤ Breathe through your nose instead of your mouth; it can extend your life.

➤ Smile at people, even strangers; it helps reduce your cortisol levels.

➤ Spend time in silence each day; stress can shorten your life more than sugar.

➤ Eat until you're 80% full; the longest-lived individuals tend to stop eating before they feel stuffed.

➤ Show love and respect to your elders; honoring them is beneficial for the soul and can have anti-aging effects.

➤ Avoid extremes in food, opinions, and lifestyle choices.

Let the fast ones burn their youth like oil. Let the loud ones chase the wind and call it power. You start to breathe slower. Chew slower. Forgive faster. Let your life stretch like bamboo, quiet, bending, enduring. To live long is not to run farther, but to resist less. This is the *Shòu* way: Long life, soft steps, clean soul.

CHAPTER 7

Rén

(仁)

COMPASSION AS YOUTHFULNESS

~~~

I looked at my eighty-eight-year-old grandma, who was carefully coloring the pages of her coloring book. It'd been several weeks since her birthday, but my mom still insisted we needed to spend as much time with her as possible since she was getting older. So, we took her to the beach because, ever since she had a leg injury, she hadn't been able to walk. She just sat in the chair with her big sunglasses, coloring in her coloring book as my mom and I spent time with her.

My mom came around the corner with three big glasses of water that she balanced with ease. As she set them down, I noticed how much younger my mom looked. She had lost weight since my visit to the emergency room, and her eyes seemed lighter.

The same thing happened with my dad. The older he gets, the younger he looks and acts. I'm beginning to see a glimpse of who my mom was as a little girl. As she set the water on the table and adjusted her sundress, which made her look like a young girl, she happily crawled into my grandma's arms while my grandma was coloring in her coloring book. She gave my grandma a big hug and kissed her many times, just like a parent would do to embarrass their child in front of their friends. I remember seeing how happy my mom was. She enjoyed the play and the laughter. I could see the weight lifted from her heart and the peace in her mind compared to before.

When my grandma was done coloring, we picked her up and slowly walked her into the ocean, dipped her in, and saw the look on her face as she got into the water.

She explained, "I never thought I was ever going to experience this ever again." She said it gratefully, a tone of sadness in her voice, but wonder in her eyes as she shrieked with laughter as a little fish touched her hand and swam away with the mountains behind her. My mom and I looked at each other, laughing.

All I saw was nature and my grandma and my mom, two women who sacrificed so much to make sure that I lived a good life, sacrificed their health, their youth, their relationships. Just to make sure that my sister and I can grow up into the people that we need to become. I noticed that the wrinkles that were once apparent on my mom in her thirties and forties seemed to have almost disappeared as she approached her sixties. Now I didn't think it was the sunscreen that she applied rigorously multiple times throughout the day. I didn't think it was the beauty regimen of creams and simple foods that she'd been eating.

I noticed a different glow in my mom, and I saw it in my dad as well: as they got older, compared to other people their age, they seemed to be getting lighter, more playful, and more childlike. While people I know in the West of a similar age tend to become rigid, inflexible, and hardened. I noticed how much love is in my mom and dad's eyes now as they are getting lighter. Every time I see them, I make an effort to fully appreciate the moment because I understand they won't be around forever. I want to soak in the compassion reflected in their eyes as they embrace their second chance at life and age gracefully.

The Chinese have a word for this. It's called *Rén (ren)*, and it means compassion as youthfulness. It's a Confucian virtue where it says kindness, not just as morality, is a medicine for the soul. When you focus on harnessing your *Rén*, you focus on compassion, emotional generosity, and relational harmony as a longevity secret. The practice is simple: daily kindness, forgiveness, rituals, and warm social connection. Now, my mom, my dad, and I spend as much time as possible together, with my sister, and with my grandparents.

As I spend more time with my mom and dad as they age, I'm starting to realize that some people develop wrinkles from frowning, while others have wrinkles from love. The main difference lies in their eyes. You can see their *Rén*. In Confucianism, it is often translated as benevolence, humaneness, or compassionate kindness, and is considered the highest virtue. It literally means 'person + two,' referring to a person in a relationship. You cannot practice *Rén* alone. It lives in how you treat others. That compassion is not considered as softness or sacrifice, but rather as a life-extending, youth-protecting force.

In Chinese medicine, emotions are believed to directly affect the body's organs. Anger is said to damage the liver, while grief can deplete the lungs. Fear is associated with weakening the kidneys, and worry is considered to burden the spleen. On the positive side, joy is thought to have a regulating effect on the heart. Each emotion plays a crucial role in maintaining the balance and health of our internal systems.

So compassion, as the antidote to resentment, bitterness, and anxiety, literally preserves your organs. And wrinkles from smiling are not the same as wrinkles from worry.

One of Chang's parables would go:

"Mike, in a small village, two elderly women lived side by side. One was always complaining. She criticized her children, the weather, and her neighbors. The other greeted everyone with warmth. She fed the stray dogs and sang to her plants. One day, a boy asked, 'Why does one look so young and the other so tired?' An elder replied, 'One woman carries her kindness on her face. The other carries her grudges in her bones.'"

Recent insights into modern wellness and longevity highlight the wisdom found in ancient teachings. Research indicates that individuals who volunteer often experience a reduced risk of mortality, while those with strong social connections tend to live longer. Additionally, forgiveness has been shown to lower cortisol levels and reduce inflammation, thereby contributing to overall health. Moreover, simple acts like smiling and laughing can release hormones that help preserve youthfulness, underscoring the interconnectedness of emotional well-being and longevity.

In blue zones, elders aren't isolated; they are integrated. A sense of "Belonging" is their skincare.

How the West Gets Compassion Wrong

Western Compassion	*Rén* (仁) Compassion
Performance (virtue signaling)	Presence (being truly with others)
Burnout caregiving	Gentle, steady kindness
Transactional kindness	Rooted, unconditional giving
Independence obsession	Interdependence as strength

The West often sees compassion as self-sacrifice to exhaustion. *Rén* is about staying kind without losing yourself. Compassion that ages you is not true *Rén*. True *Rén* softens the face and strengthens the soul. Compassion must be trained like a muscle.

How to Apply *Rén* in Daily Life:

➤ Practice soft eye contact. See people as souls, not problems.

➤ Forgive before sleep. Release emotional tension.

➤ Use warm language. Not just polite words, but kind tones.

➤ Spend time with those who feel like sunlight.

➤ Serve someone weekly with no expectation in return.

➤ Even a smile is medicine.

Essential Habits for Compassion as Anti-Aging:

➤ Say "thank you" often and mean it.

➤ Bless people silently in your mind. It rewires your heart.

➤ Turn judgment into curiosity.

➤ Spend time with animals or children. They train softness.

➤ Write one kind message each day to someone or to yourself.

➤ Avoid gossip. It pollutes the skin and spirit.

➤ Ask one deep question in every conversation.

➤ Connect soul to soul.

Kindness keeps the soul clean. And clean souls rarely age. The hands that *give* age slower. The heart that *forgives* beats longer. The face that *smiles more* needs no surgery. *Rén* is not about being nice. It's about living in a way that makes even strangers feel a little more at home in the world. May your kindness be your mirror. May your gentleness be your glow.

CHAPTER 8

Dào

(道)

RETURNING TO SIMPLICITY

———— ~~~ ————

I look up to my little sister, that same little baby in the beginning of the book that was looking up at the ceiling, crying with me when I first found out about death. I didn't realize that, as I got older, she would eventually also become my best friend, as did my mom and my dad. You see, the reason I look up to her is that she is unlike me, who has essentially forced a lot of things in my life. I would either chase a career or a relationship. I sought better health as a way to gain control, but in doing so, I often ended up hurt, overwhelmed, and burnt out repeatedly. I had to learn the hard way what it truly means to find balance and embrace simplicity.

My sister understood innately what it means to follow the *Dào* (dow), or, as the ancient Chinese philosophy of Taoism calls it, "the way." When she was in college, she knew immediately she didn't want to be a nurse. My parents tried to force her into a career, just like they tried to make me a dentist. However, my sister immediately knew that being a nurse was not for her.

So, immediately, she looked deep inside her heart and realized what her *Dào* was. What is her way? What are the things that she doesn't want to chase? What are the things that she wants to return to? I'm amazed at how much wisdom she had in identifying her values. Her values included letting go of stress, reducing excess ambition, and embracing a natural flow in life. She believed in living simply, prioritizing health, maintaining a healthy diet, and fostering open communication with a partner. When she looked deep into her heart, she chose to change her path. Instead of chasing goals like I did, she wanted to connect with her inner child and understand what she really wanted.

Without forcing it, she found herself naturally drawn to Asia, leaving America. She naturally found the right community that was into spirituality, wellness, health, nutrition, and design. She gave without expecting anything in return. When she was running out of money in Thailand, my mom and dad worried that their little daughter might get hurt. But my sister always had a strong trust in the natural flow of life.

I was always amazed by how she never got stressed to the point of imploding, like I did. She always knew when to relax when things got too intense. She always knew when to rest when things got too stressful. Because of that, she never really had to deal with the exact same issues that I had. I remember a time when we were talking, and she expressed her worries about running out of money in Thailand.

She was uncertain about how she would earn a living, where the universe was leading her, or what her future plans were.

I remember her expressing all those worries in tears, but not tears of being a victim. Tears of allowing any strong emotion inside to be fully expressed, not repressed, so it wouldn't control her. They were almost like sweet tears as they rolled down her face, shedding all of the pain from trying to latch onto her nervous system and just fully letting it go.

At first, I was confused. I thought she was emotional. Little did I know, there was a lot of wisdom in how she expressed her emotions so that they weren't repressed. She expressed her emotions so that they weren't repressed in her body like mine were. After that conversation, she was able to calm down and establish a deep level of trust within herself. No matter what challenges arose, she returned to her core values, never chased after excessive ambition, and consistently let go of stress to flow with the natural rhythm of life. She maintained an abundance mindset, generously giving to those around her.

As a result, she began attracting health and wellness clients, yoga studios, health experts, doctors, and chiropractors who sought her branding and design services. Unlike me, she never overworked or overextended herself. Instead, she effortlessly attracted clients who resonated with her heart, values, and soul. She had clients she truly enjoyed working with.

Her branding and design business became successful not by chasing, but by returning to herself and realigning with who she was. It's a lesson I learned from my sister, because no matter how many times life goes up and down for her, as it does for everyone, she's never afraid to healthily express her feelings and not let them control her. And she always gave to her clients without expecting anything in return. And every single time life seemed to be getting worse for her, it would always swing back in her favor because she was always in flow.

Not only that, but she was able to balance that with her health, her nutrition, her time with her family, our mom and dad. She is a perfect example of what Chinese wisdom refers to as the *Dào*, or "the way." This concept represents a path that encourages us not to chase after things, but rather to return to a state of simplicity. It emphasizes living in harmony with nature, embracing its ebbs and flows, and accepting life's ups and downs. It teaches us to let go of stress during difficult times and to release ambition and excess during times of prosperity.

You see, life is always a mix of ups and downs. Life isn't always positive, but it isn't always negative either. Life is a balance of the good and the bad. But the secret of the *Dào* that I learned from my sister, as she channels natural Chinese energy through her blood, deep in our ancestry, from Filipino roots, she always knows how to ebb and flow whenever life doesn't seem to go her way. I've seen it time and time again.

I also see it in her partner, Pete. Pete began his journey in a small rural area of the UK with humble beginnings. He always knew deep in his heart who he was, the values he held, and the man he would become. In contrast to me, he never really had to chase after his dreams. He always understood what was important to him and what his values were. This clarity led him to leave his small town in his early twenties, backpacking across India and living out of a backpack as he followed his adventurous spirit.

He then continued his journey to Vietnam, where he experienced the same lifestyle, ultimately winding up in Thailand. He's someone who also breathes the natural flow of the *Dào* in his veins. He attracts the right people, business opportunities, and product ideas with ease. Together, both Pete and my sister are perfect examples of what it means to follow the *Dào* and the natural flow of life.

When nothing is forced, the universe essentially gives you what it is that you want. Now, here's the thing about the universe. The universe has existed far longer than we have lived. Here I was, a human being, thinking I could control the universe and have it bend to my will.

If you just tap into the *Dào* in the center of balance in the natural flow of life, and you ride the *Dào* like how a surfer rides a wave, what happens is the universe is actually trying to swing life in your favor. Letting go was the hardest thing for me. However, seeing Angelique and Pete fully embrace it, I realize how impactful the *Dào* is.

Take my situation, for example. I tried to find my peace by moving all around the world in search of happiness. I have tried living in South America, Europe, Bali, and Thailand. I was always anxious about staying in one place, thinking that I needed to find life elsewhere, never realizing that my insecurities would follow me wherever I went. While I was chasing different countries in search of my home, Angelique and Pete stamped their flag on the floor in a small city in Thailand. Everything they desired was constructed around them, rather than them pursuing it.

For example, I love purple sweet potatoes, or purple "*kamotes*" in the Philippines. I like moving to places where they have purple *kamote* because that's what the people in the blue zones eat to live long. So,

I always bounce around. My sister and Pete live in an area where there's an abundance of purple *kamote*. Another thing: I like going to places with saunas and ice baths. So I always move to different parts of the city where they have these. My sister and Pete didn't move, and an ice bath and sauna got built right down the street from them.

I really like going to nice gyms so I can exercise and do calisthenics, handstands, cartwheels, and rings. There was this beautiful gym in Bali that I would go to. It was perfect. I was like, "There's never going to be anything like this in the world." My sister and Pete just stayed at their home. Lo and behold, the most amazing gym was built right next to their house. I cannot explain it to you. My sister and Pete live so much in the *Dào*, living so simply, yet so abundantly; they literally stay in their center, and the world comes to them. When you do not force the universe, the universe ends up giving back to you tenfold.

In times of stress, pain, and hardship, if you don't fight with the universe, and you learn to let go, the universe will swing back in your favor if you don't react. Lao Tzu wrote in the *Tao Te Ching*, "When nothing is done, nothing is left undone."

Now, this doesn't mean laziness; it means non-resistance, letting nature, your body, and your soul return to balance without overcontrol. In Taoism, longevity comes not from biohacking but from non-striving. You don't stretch the flower to make it grow; you water it, then you trust the process.

How you do that is not by "hustling." Chinese longevity villages are not full of hustle and bustle. They are full of sunrise walking, gardens, herbs, tea, and jokes with neighbors. The Way or the *Dào* is not a technique. It's a rhythm. A slowing down to the point where your body remembers: Youth is not something to chase. It's something that arrives when stress leaves. That's what Pete and Angelique seem to get right every day. They take a sunrise walk, have plants in their home, drink herbs and teas regularly, joke with their neighbors, and aren't afraid to slow down. I need to take a page from their book. Which is why I sleep on their couch every couple of months to be reminded of what the *Dào* is (Thanks, Pete and Angelique, if you're reading this, haha).

It reminds me of a parable Chang would tell me. "A man once traveled across China searching for the secret to long life. He met monks who gave him herbs, doctors who gave him pills, and scholars who gave him formulas. Decades passed. His back bent. His beard whitened. One day, on the brink of death, he entered a quiet village and met a smiling one-hundred-year-old woman making tea. He asked, 'What's your secret?' She said, 'I sleep early. I sit in the sun. I love my chickens. And I never rushed a single day of my life.'"

Modern science confirms that activities like forest bathing (immersing yourself in the forest) reduce cortisol levels. Grounding (barefoot walking) reduces inflammation. Early sunlight regulates sleep and hormones. Simplicity reduces decision fatigue and increases well-being. Rural elders who maintain strong routines tend to live longer and happier lives. Minimalism isn't just aesthetic. It's biological.

How the West Gets Simplicity Wrong

Western Minimalism	Taoist Simplicity (*Dào*)
Sterile, white, cold design	Earthy, natural, alive
Productivity through fewer tasks	Peace through fewer desires

Decluttering homes	Emptying the heart
Escaping stress through structure	Dissolving stress through trust

In the West, simplicity is often just a new way to optimize. But *Dào* is not optimization. It's alignment, letting your soul breathe.

How to Apply *Dào* in Daily Life:

➢ Wake up with the sun, not alarms.

➢ Walk barefoot on grass each morning.

➢ Let go of one unnecessary ambition.

➢ Tend to something living: a plant, a pet, a child.

➢ Disconnect from digital noise at least one day a week.

➢ Eat one meal without distractions.

➢ Just chew and be.

➢ Simplicity is the ultimate youth serum.

Essential Habits for Taoist Simplicity:

➢ Morning stillness before screens.

➢ Touching the earth with bare feet.

➢ Listening to wind or birds instead of music.

➢ Replacing multitasking with mono-tasking.

➢ Gardening, sweeping, or quiet chores as active meditation.

➢ Drinking clean water slowly (not gulping energy drinks).

➢ Letting go of "shoulds" in exchange for "what's true now."

➤ Spending time with elders who laugh more than they talk.

You do not need more to become more. You only need to return. Return to the earth beneath your feet. The water in your cup. The softness in your breath. The *Dào* is not a secret path. It is the one your soul already knows. Take your time. You are not behind. You are being guided back to the way that keeps you young.

CHAPTER 9

Tea and Tonic Herbs:

THE DAILY RITUALS OF RENEWAL

I was sitting on the floor late in the evening in a deep Asian squat, visualizing the poop coming out of my intestines, and relaxing to see if I could have a bowel movement as I closed my eyes in my sister's living room. Because my poop consistency had been very, very bad, on and off, depending on how much I controlled and how much I let go, my sister asked me, "What are you doing?" I was like, "I'm trying to have my daily poop, and I didn't go today." And she was like, "Let me make you tea." I'm like, "Tea? Why tea?" Then she told me that everything's better with tea. She went into the kitchen and made a special tea with natural ingredients, brewing it in hot water.

She yelled from the kitchen, "Mike, what do you want?" and I said, "I want to get good sleep, be able to poop, relax, and stay calm."

She said, "I have the perfect fix." I heard interesting grinding noises coming from the kitchen, which was her laboratory of natural nutrition creations, from teas and meals to natural electrolyte concoctions. She liked going in there and combining a lot of natural ingredients to fit whatever her needs are. The day before, when we were playing pickleball, it was electrolytes.

Now, today, as I was trying to visualize the perfect poop, it was evening tea. She gave me this amazing-smelling concoction in a cute little mug that said "gratitude" on it. Looking at it, my heart warmed with joy as I realized that what I had in my hand was a perfect fix to what I'd been searching for. I looked at her with tears in my eyes, saying, "Thank you, Angelique."

She looked at me and said, "You're weird," smiled, and went back into the kitchen.

You see, in Chinese longevity culture, the most powerful medicine is brewed. It's not prescribed. From green tea to ginseng to goji to reishi, tonic herbs aren't trends. They're quiet allies that fortify the spirit and preserve youth. The main focus of Chinese philosophy is embracing food as medicine, daily micro-rituals, and gentle herbal nutrition and nourishment as a foundation for lifelong vitality. That's what my sister and all of her clients in the health and wellness space do to maintain vitality, especially as they age.

It's nothing synthetic; it begins with simple, time-tested tonics that have survived for thousands of years. Not some random product created recently, but something that has stood the test of time. Now, when I consume things, I ask myself whether they pass the five-hundred-year test. When I eat or drink anything, I ask myself, "Am I consuming something that is in its natural form that was also consumed five hundred years ago?" If something isn't healthy, it's best to avoid it. However, beverages like green tea, goji berry water, ginseng tea, and reishi have been part of Chinese culture for thousands of years. Establishing a daily ritual of sipping these drinks is one of the simplest ways to promote youthfulness.

Now, in the Chinese culture we talked about earlier, known as *Yǎng Shēng*, the art of daily life nourishment, tonics aren't used to treat sickness. They're used to prevent depletion. These herbs don't force the body; they guide it towards balance. Because the best doctor is actually preventing the disease before it arises, not after you have already experienced the pain.

When compared with modern wellness, they chase spikes. High-dose IV drips, biohacks, detox extremes, but Chinese medicine plays the long game. Small sips, long effects. Daily quiet tonics instead of crisis pills, and cumulative vitality, not explosive highs. Youthfulness is preserved slowly, like tea steeping.

Chang's Parable: A young man once asked a master how to gain energy. The master replied, "Drink this tea." The boy refused, insisting, "Give me something stronger!" Years later, after experiencing burnout and breakdown, he returned to the master. To his surprise, the master was still drinking the same tea and continuing to walk the hills with ease.

The Modern Wellness Comparison

Modern Health	Tonic Herbalism
Caffeine spikes	Gentle stimulation
Pharmaceuticals	Food-grade healing
Trendy powders	Timeless plants
Reactive	Preventative
Outsourced to doctors	Personal ritual

Daily Tonic Allies: Gentle, Safe, and Timeless

Green Tea (*Lu Cha*): Green tea is an antioxidant powerhouse that promotes digestion, liver health, and clear skin. It's a great choice to drink in the morning or early afternoon.

Goji Berries (*Gou Qi Zi*): These berries serve as a blood tonic, offering eye support and enhancing skin vitality. They can be steeped in hot water and sipped throughout the day.

Ginseng (*Ren Shen*): As an adaptogen, ginseng boosts *Qi*, stamina, and the immune system. It's best consumed in the mornings or during cold seasons. However, it's recommended to use it only when feeling depleted, rather than daily for everyone.

Reishi Mushroom (*Ling Zhi*): Reishi mushroom is known as a *Shén* tonic, calming the spirit and supporting sleep and immunity. It can be taken before bed as a tea or in a capsule.

Schisandra Berries (*Wu Wei Zi*): These five-flavor berries help balance organs and tone *Qi* while supporting skin health, mental clarity, and hormone balance.

You don't need a cabinet full of herbs; starting with one is sufficient. Build a ritual around it; a quiet moment with a mug of meaning. Let it serve as your morning calm before the world begins, your afternoon grounding between tasks, or your evening exhale before sleep.

Habits to Cultivate the Ritual of Herbal Youth: To enhance your herbal experience, keep your favorite tonic herbs visible in your kitchen, creating a tea altar. Use a beautiful mug or teapot to elevate the moment and make it feel sacred. Take the time to learn the energetics of each herb, whether they are warming, cooling, or calming. Rotate your selections based on the season or your energy levels. Lastly, sip slowly, without distraction, allowing the ritual to help you slow down.

The secret to youth is not force. It's fortification. With each sip, you remind your body: You are being taken care of. You are treasured. You are tuned. Tea doesn't shout. It whispers, "Live slowly. Heal gently. The path to youth is brewed one cup at a time."

CHAPTER 10

Jīng

(精)

VITAL ESSENCE

———∾———

I woke up to little whiskers tickling my cheek. As my eyes opened, it felt like I'd been asleep for eternity. My sister's cat, Bandit, licked me awake. The sun was just rising, and already I had to go to the bathroom. I rushed and had the smoothest bowel movement ever. It looked like my sister's tea tonic the night before really did hit the spot.

As I came out of their guest bedroom, I walked downstairs, but just as I was going down, I heard giggling from my mom and dad's room in the other guest bedroom. I covered my ears and pretended not to hear. I couldn't help but laugh and chuckle at my parents at seventy-two and fifty-eight years old, still giggling in the early mornings. I went downstairs and noticed Bandit's scratch toy was peeling up all over the floor. I grabbed the broom and the dustpan, and I slowly cleaned them, as if that morning wasn't a meditation. I then organized the shoes and put all of the drying plates into the cabinets. Now, while I was in the kitchen, I noticed my dad walking down a little bit after me, already ready for his morning *tai chi*. He looked at me and smiled. I looked at him, shaking my head in funny disbelief at how playful my dad was this early in the morning.

I noticed his essence was much livelier than when I was younger. As he's already doing the fish dance, he's preparing his morning movements. I saw my mom follow shortly after, and I noticed her essence was different. How they literally radiated with so much life force compared to when I was younger. You know, it's like, I remember looking at my mom and dad when I was in college and thinking they literally wouldn't live much longer.

The stress of the work, the double shifts as a nurse, the late-night hours, and the long train rides going to the city for my dad. When I was younger, I actually had this fear that my parents were only going to live for five more years because of the stress at their jobs. They were extremely overworked. They were highly stressed. There was so much emotional chaos from the house foreclosure to the threats of divorce. They were fully caffeinated. They were tired. They were empty.

As I see them now, I see so much more life force in them than I did when I was younger. As I see them now, I see so much more life in their eyes. If you were to put a picture of what they looked like ten years ago, compared to what they look like now, you would think the picture of them ten years ago would be what they looked like as they aged. Because now they look even younger than they looked ten years ago, with all the stress.

Now, how is this possible? In Chinese medicine, it's known as *Jīng (jing).* It's your original essence, your deepest life force. It's stored in the kidneys and passed down from your parents. My parents' *Jīng* was passed down to them from their parents. Due to significant family trauma, their *Jīng* has been depleting rapidly since an early age because of all the stress. You see, my mom grew up in the Philippines, where they had no money.

My grandma's mom was slightly crazy and lived in a jail cell. No matter how crazy my grandma's mom was, my grandma loved her wholeheartedly. But the stress of finances and family drama really had my mom inherit a lot of drama, which sucked away her *Jīng.* My aunt shared stories about how much my grandma and grandpa fought, including one incident where my grandma sprayed my grandpa with pepper spray. This behavior, which my mom also inherited, drained her *Jīng* even further. Additionally, having to leave her home and move to America without a support system while raising two kids further depleted her *Jīng.*

My dad, same thing. Growing up, he was in the Philippines. He had to sell things on the street and find creative ways to earn some extra money. That's where his entrepreneurial spirit really began. He had to go ahead and make money to support his family at an early age. On top of that, he lost a bunch of money right when he thought he would keep it forever.

When he lost everything, he got married and started a family. Moving to America shortly after and having only $500 to their name in a new country where people could barely understand my parents' English, my mom and dad both had deep-seated traumatic experiences that drained their *Jīng.* Already, they were handicapped with their life force at the start of childhood and especially at the start of adulthood. That is why they looked so old in pictures, even in their forties.

Now, seeing them, I know that they were able to reverse the effects of all the stress. And to preserve it and protect it and cultivate it through rest, restraint, nutrition, and emotional balance. Through deep sleeping, discipline, herbal tonics, breathing practices, and letting go of energy leaks and toxic people in their lives. My parents, as I see them before me, are aging backward.

Now, the thing about *Jīng* is that you cannot buy it. It's something you lose slowly, unless you protect it like sacred oil. *Jīng* is one of the Three Treasures in Taoist and Traditional Chinese Medicine:

Jīng (精) – Essence

Qì (氣) – Energy

Shén (神) – Spirit

Jīng is your deepest vitality stored in the kidneys. You receive it from your parents (pre-natal *Jīng*) and can cultivate or deplete it through how you live (post-natal *Jīng*).

When *Jīng* is strong, you age gracefully, you feel steady, fertile, and rooted, you glow without needing makeup or stimulants. When it's weak, hair falls or grays early, you feel scattered, sexually drained, or unmotivated. You have chronic fatigue or poor immunity, which creeps in. The modern world burns through *Jīng* like gasoline. Every all-nighter, sexual excess, binge-watch, argument, or ultra-processed food draws from your core essence. Chinese longevity culture teaches the opposite: Restraint, stillness, tonics, deep rest, and quiet joy. *Jīng* isn't about doing more. It's about leaking less.

Another Chang Parable: "There once was a man admired for his spark. He was charming, sexual, ambitious, and burned through life fast. By forty, his back ached. His spirit dimmed. He looked older than his father. He sought help from a Taoist sage who handed him a candle. 'This is your *Jīng*,' the sage said. 'You can burn it with glory or guard it with grace. Either way, once it's gone, it's gone.' He learned to live like a lantern, glowing steady, not blazing wild."

Western equivalents of *Jīng* might include adrenal health, mitochondrial function, hormonal balance, deep sleep cycles, sexual energy, hair and nail health, fertility, and healthy bones. Many youth-preserving protocols (like collagen, magnesium, rest, zinc, and herbal tonics) trace back to *Jīng* cultivation. While the West often focuses on surface symptoms, Traditional Chinese Medicine targets the core energy.

How the West Gets Vitality Wrong

Western Health Philosophy	Taoist Jīng Wisdom
Push harder, take supplements	Do less, protect what you have
Burn energy for productivity	Store energy for longevity
"You only live once." Expend it all	"Preserve essence." Live long and steady
Pleasure chasing = freedom	Pleasure control = youth preservation
Stimulants and hacks	Sleep, stillness, and herbs

The West teaches you to extract more from your body. The East teaches you to guard the wellspring.

How to Apply *Jīng* Wisdom in Your Daily Life:

➤ Sleep is sacred. Your kidneys and adrenals recover only in deep rest.

➤ Don't overstimulate. Limit caffeine, blue light, and constant socializing.

➤ Practice sexual discipline. Especially for men: semen retention or spacing ejaculations builds *Jīng*.

➤ Eat *Jīng*-nourishing foods: black sesame, goji berries, bone broth, kidney beans, walnuts, eggs.

➤ Use *Jīng* tonics: Rehmannia, He Shou Wu, Schisandra, Dang Gui, Cordyceps.

➤ Meditate or breathe deeply, *qìgōng*-style, to circulate energy instead of leaking it.

➤ Avoid drama, overreactions, and grudges. They drain your spirit.

What are Rehmannia, He Shou Wu, Schisandra, Dang Gui, and Cordyceps in Traditional Chinese Medicine (TCM)?

Rehmannia (*Shu Di Huang* / 生地黄)

Type: Root (usually prepared by steaming in wine).
Functions in TCM: Nourishes *yin*, replenishes blood, supports kidney and liver essence.
Traditional Uses: Fatigue, dizziness, tinnitus, diabetes-like thirst, menopause, anemia.
Modern Notes: Sometimes compared to a natural "adrenal tonic" because it's thought to restore depleted energy reserves.

He Shou Wu (*Fo-Ti* / 何首乌)

<u>Type</u>: Root (Polygonum multiflorum).

<u>Functions in TCM</u>: Famous "longevity herb" that nourishes blood, supports hair growth, and strengthens the kidney and liver.

<u>Traditional Uses:</u> Premature graying, hair loss, fertility, fatigue, sexual vitality.

<u>Modern Notes</u>: Raw form is toxic; prepared form is used medicinally. Often marketed as an anti-aging tonic.

Schisandra (*Wu Wei Zi* / 五味子)

<u>Type</u>: Berry ("five-flavor fruit").

<u>Functions in TCM</u>: Astringes and preserves *Qi*, calms the spirit, supports the lungs, kidneys, and liver.

<u>Traditional Uses</u>: Improves endurance, enhances concentration, helps with cough, night sweats, and stress.

<u>Modern Notes</u>: Considered an adaptogen, supporting stress resilience and liver detoxification.

Dang Gui (*Angelica Sinensis* / 当归)

<u>Type</u>: Root (often called "female ginseng").

<u>Functions in TCM</u>: Tonifies and invigorates blood, regulates menstruation, alleviates pain.

<u>Traditional Uses</u>: Women's health, menstrual irregularities, fatigue from blood deficiency, and circulation issues.

<u>Modern Notes</u>: Often included in formulas for women's vitality, though also used for both men and women as a general blood tonic.

Cordyceps (*Dong Chong Xia Cao* / 冬虫夏草)

Type: Medicinal fungus (grows on caterpillars in the wild; most modern supply is cultivated).

Functions in TCM: Tonifies kidney *yang*, boosts essence and lung *Qi*.

Traditional Uses: Chronic fatigue, kidney weakness, weak lungs (asthma, chronic cough), low libido.

Modern Notes: Popular among athletes for improving stamina, oxygen utilization, and immune support.

Habits That Cultivate (or Destroy) *Jīng*

Jīng-Building Habits

➤ Deep sleep before 11 p.m.

➤ Breathwork or stillness daily

➤ Eating warm, cooked, nutrient-rich meals

➤ Drinking herbal tonics for the kidneys

➤ Hot foot soaks before bed

➤ Gentle *qìgōng* or *tai chi*

➤ Releasing toxic relationships or drama

➤ Sexual restraint or mindful intimacy

Jīng-Draining Habits

➤ Late-night scrolling

➤ Smoking, drinking, overstimulation

➤ Processed foods and cold/raw diet

➤ Frequent emotional outbursts

➤ Sleep deprivation

➤ Excessive ejaculation or sexual indulgence

➤ Constant stimulation via nootropics or pre-workouts

You were not meant to burn out. You were meant to glow. *Jīng* is the sacred oil inside your lamp. Protect it. Guard it from the winds of chaos. Let it shine slow, soft, eternal. For it is not the loudest flame that lasts, but the one that stays lit long after the others have flickered away.

CHAPTER 11

Shén

(神)

RADIANT SPIRIT

~~~~

I yelled out the door late in the evening, "Dad, it's time to come back. Dinner is almost ready, and it's getting late."

My dad yelled back, "Five more minutes," as he bobbed up and down in his bright orange life jacket, wearing a bright blue rash guard, looking like a little boy with his goggles and snorkel on, swimming joyfully with his childhood friend. Now, his childhood friend is someone I call 'uncle,' even though we're not related by blood. He's someone who has taught me many valuable life lessons. Growing up, he lost his father at the age of nine. His mother, as a single parent, did her best to raise him. However, shortly after that, she was struck by a devastating illness that left her unable to think or care for herself.

So, before the age of thirteen, my uncle had to be the family's breadwinner. He had to find a way to provide for his mom and his siblings, but, with no father figure or role model, he was constantly grasping at straws for answers. As I watched my uncle and my dad bobbing up and down, laughing like little boys, I noticed my uncle's bald head, with wispy hair around it, much like what grandpas often have. He looks more Chinese than my dad because his parents came from mainland China to the Philippines.

As I watched my dad and my uncle, both wearing their bubbly oversized life jackets and rash guards, I saw them laughing, singing, and playing together. They kept saying "five more minutes" over and over as they enjoyed each other's company, playfully bobbing up and down without a care in the world, completely oblivious to the fact that dinner was getting cold. In that moment, I finally understood why my uncle had always shared Chinese parables and wisdom with me since I was young.

The more I learned about my uncle, the more I realized he had nothing else to fall back on but the Chinese wisdom he had learned from books and his faith in a higher power. With those things alone, he was able to crawl out of extreme poverty, trauma, pain, and burden, and was able to become highly successful to the level where the resort that we were staying at for free was literally his. He owned this huge beachfront property in the Philippines, where scuba divers from all around the world come and visit. He had hotels, properties, and businesses across different hotel chains. He was able to build a vast amount of wealth, but when I looked at him, I didn't see any of that. I saw my uncle, who got a lot of joy pretending to be a homeless man, going up to the security guard at one of his hotels, asking the security guard, "Oh, this is a nice building. What's inside?" testing the security guard and the security guard shooing my uncle away, thinking he's a homeless man or a beggar.

My uncle just walked away, laughing and smiling, the security guard not even realizing that he just shooed away the owner. My uncle is an excellent example not just of how to make wealth from nothing, but also of how to hold it. Because many people I know came from wealthy upbringings, I remember seeing their families and kids surrounded by beauty, luxury, lights, and laughter. I remember when I was younger, I would always compare myself to the rich kids in school, thinking, *Why can't I be like them? Why does my family have to be in so much pain?*

The older I became and the closer I looked, I noticed something behind the eyes of those who pursue luxury, power, and status. When you looked closer, there was something inside of them that almost felt empty. Not my uncle, who dressed up as a homeless man. When he had a hole in his shirt, his wife got angry and said, "Why don't you just buy another shirt?" And my uncle just sewed it himself and wore it. My uncle, who wore the white T-shirt with clear yellow stains around the armpits, not caring, laughing, singing, and dancing.

My uncle, whose kids grew up with such good character. I asked his daughter, who's a couple of years older than me, "How were you raised where you guys are so good?"

She looked at me, deadpan in the face, saying, "I didn't know our family was wealthy until I was in my mid-twenties because my mom and dad were always so humble."

When I look deep into his eyes, his wife's eyes, his daughter's eyes, and his two sons' eyes, I see a family that was raised with ancient Chinese philosophy dancing in their veins. For the amount of wealth that they have, when I look in their eyes, there's something warm, alive, soft, and bright compared to other people. The eyes of someone praised for their appearance seem flawless on the outside, but their spirit feels dim, distracted, and exhausted.

That's when I realized that youth is not in the skin, it's in the spirit. This is *Shén (shen)*, as it is called in Traditional Chinese Medicine. It represents your spirit, housed in the heart, your presence, clarity, emotional tone, and your inner light. Where the focus is on true beauty and on youth coming from within peace, presence, and spiritual depth. And by stillness, spiritual devotion, avoiding over-stimulation, and cultivating joy and presence. It creates a spirit that shines through the eyes and face, unbuyable and unmistakable.

That's what I see when I look at my uncle, my aunt, their daughter, and their two sons. My uncle doesn't use sunscreen or take supplements. Even at seventy-two years old, he still drinks and smokes, which is different from my dad. However, among all of my dad's friends who pursued wealth, he is the only one who remains skinny, lively, and joyful, with a lightness in his face and eyes. He's the only one who has strong relationships with his kids. He's the only one who's humble and pretends to be homeless to prevent overstimulation from robbing his youth. And he's my dad's best friend.

I remember meeting my uncle for the first time when I was ten years old. My dad said, back when we were living in the Midwest, "My best friend's coming. He's your uncle."

I was like, "Who?"

"Yeah, his son's going to sleep in your room. You're going to share the bunk bed." And when he walked in the door, my dad's best friend, I saw this man with a bald head and hair growing out of the sides, kind of like a mad scientist, with a family that didn't look like mine. They looked like they had deep Chinese descent, but my dad said that he was born and raised in the Philippines.

It was amazing to see this man living in my grandma's old room with his wife. His daughter lived with my sister in her room, and the two sons stayed in my room. That week, my dad took me out of school, and we just spent quality time together.

The daughter taught me how to solve complicated puzzles, like a big sister would do. I was like, "Wow, she's a genius." The sons, I would watch TV with them all the time, and we would play outside. As I went downstairs, some mornings I'd see him washing the dishes or sweeping the floors with pure humility.

I remember that week was a very beautiful moment when my mom and dad didn't fight or threaten each other about divorce. That week, all I felt was a deep sense of peace. Now, looking back, I realize they brought Chinese wisdom and embodied it in our family for that moment. In that moment, I experienced firsthand what happens when you truly have a philosophy in life, one that's intertwined with your family. I felt what true *Shén* feels like. I remember the emptiness that I felt when they left.

As they left for the airport, I waved goodbye, crying because I had just made best friends with their kids. My dad nudged the corner of my shoulder. He said, "Son, do you know that man is one of the wealthiest people I know?"

In my mind, I was shocked because I thought he was just some simple man. Here's a man who had amazing *Shén*. Now, *Shén* is the last of the three treasures in Chinese medicine. *Jīng* is your essence, your battery. *Qi* is your energy, which is your current. *Shén* is your spirit, which is your consciousness.

Shén animates your expressions, your voice, your joy, and your presence. You've seen someone who glows with love, laughter, and peace. You've seen someone who's looked drained, bitter, or chaotic. Same skincare, different *Shén*.

The Taoists and sages of old didn't care about superficial youth. They asked, "Do your eyes sparkle? Do people feel peace in your presence? Are you kind when no one's watching? Because the spirit colors the face. And unlike collagen, it cannot be faked."

A Chang parable: "A beautiful woman feared aging. She spent fortunes on creams, surgeries, and photoshoots. But no matter how she tried to preserve her looks, her loneliness grew. One day, she met a blind poet. He touched her hands and said, 'Your voice feels tired. Your spirit feels hungry.' She was shaken. He couldn't see her appearance, only her essence. She returned to the mountains, fasted, prayed, and laughed with children. She found joy again. Years later, her face had aged. But people said she'd never been more radiant."

In modern science and spiritual practice, *Shén* might appear as mindfulness and meditation, heart rate variability (HRV), vagus nerve activation, calm, regulated nervous system, emotional regulation, joyful relationships, and spiritual maturity. Western wellness calls it "nervous system healing" or "presence." Chinese philosophy simply says to protect your *Shén*.

Mainstream View vs. _Shén_ Wisdom

Western Culture	Shén Wisdom (Spirit-centered aging)
Anti-aging = Botox, serums, filters	Radiance = inner calm, joy, love
Hustle, stimulation, constant engagement	Simplicity, presence, devotion
Youth as appearance	Youth as glow from within
Emotions are private, ignored	Emotions reflect spirit, must be honored
Disconnect mind-body-spirit	Integrate heart, spirit, and intention

Modern culture hides the soul. _Shén_ invites you to shine.

How to Apply _Shén_ Wisdom:

➤ Guard your heart, both emotionally and energetically.

➤ Avoid overstimulation, loud environments, screens, and gossip.

➤ Cultivate stillness and awe, morning prayer, tea ceremony, quiet walks.

➤ Laugh with loved ones, as joyful spirit strengthens your radiance.

➤ Pray or meditate, spiritual practice builds spiritual light.

➤ Watch your inner tone, as bitterness clouds the spirit,

gratitude polishes it.

Keeping my inner tone in check was my biggest problem. I noticed that when I observed the thoughts that would hang out in my mind, it was kind of like hearing the voice you hear in your head right now as you read this sentence, even though you aren't even talking. That voice that sounds like your voice. I observe that voice when I am alone and the room is quiet, and all I can hear is the buzz of the fan or the loudness of the piercing silence. I notice my inner tone and how I talk to myself is filled with a lot of anger, hatred, guilt, and shame.

When I hear that voice in my mind, I hear things like, "I am so stupid, why am I so ugly? Why am I not where I want to be? How come I don't have what I want yet? Why am I so insecure? Why am I so desperate for the approval of others? Why can't I say no? Why am I stuck in my life?" I notice that this inner tone really puts me in a disempowered state and attacks my *Shén*. Learning how to breathe love in that voice and realizing it's not my voice and letting it go, the concepts that I wrote about in *Set Boundaries: The Japanese Secret to Saying No Without Guilt and Finally Putting Yourself First*, the more I blessed that inner child inside me that craved to just be loved and seen, the more my *Shén* started thriving.

Here are other habits that strengthen (or drain) *Shén*.

Shén-Nourishing Habits:

- ➤ Morning stillness before tech
- ➤ Prayer, breathwork, or scripture
- ➤ Low-light evenings, candle-lit spaces
- ➤ Time in nature, noticing beauty

➤ Soulful, kind conversation

➤ Soft, sacred music or silence

➤ Heart-opening acts (gratitude, forgiveness)

Shén-Draining Habits:

➤ Constant noise, news, notifications

➤ Holding grudges or bitterness

➤ Overworking, screen overload

➤ Shallow or chaotic social scenes

➤ Numbing with substances or distraction

➤ Disconnection from purpose or God

You were born with light in your eyes. Not the light from screens, but the fire of your soul. Let your voice soften. Let your heart speak. Let your presence glow without trying, for beauty fades. *Shén*, the spirit that lives through the heart, makes you unforgettable.

CHAPTER 12

Xiào

(孝)

FILIAL PIETY AND FAMILY BONDS

~m~

Y ou got her?" Pete asked with a slight grunt in his voice as he held the front end of my grandma's wheelchair. I was on the other end, and my grandma was sitting in it, making it feel like we were on one of those mall rides that move back and forth.

I responded, "Yeah, Pete, I got her." I felt a bit awkward as I tried to walk backward. We had taken my grandma, who is in her late eighties, up two flights of stairs to reach the restaurant where we were having dinner. Joining us were my dad's best friend, my uncle, my grandma, Pete, Angelique, my mom, my dad, my cousins, and my uncle's children. I felt a little pain in my lower back, and I realized I was getting a little bit old as I tried to deadlift my grandma up the two flights of stairs.

Pete looked like he was having an easier time than I was, as he took the majority of my grandma's weight, while my grandma just waved her hand, smiling and laughing and giggling, like a little girl being thrown up in the air, like a superhero. My sister, mom, aunt, and my uncle's daughter just looked at us, blushing, shaking their heads, and smiling at how ridiculous the sight was.

"Left, right, left, right," Pete and I monotonously repeated as we tried to help my grandma up a winding set of stairs. After what felt like a good ten minutes, with a bit of sweat and a lot of laughter, we finally managed to get her to the top of the Chala, where we were going to have dinner at my uncle's resort, overlooking a stunning view.

It was beautiful. The sunset painted the sky in deep, vibrant oranges that contrasted beautifully with the ocean's blue. The scene calmed both the mind and the soul, while the tribal designs on the roof and the native artistry of the vast wooden bamboo structure reminded me of how a home should be built in harmony with nature.

After a long, tiring day of family time, I finally rolled my grandma over to the dinner table.

In the morning, we all ended up waking up at 4 a.m. and got into a little van, driving to a secret spot where whale sharks would come out early in the morning to catch their breakfast. We arrived at the beach early, before anyone else, and helped my grandma onto a little *banka*, a small fishing boat used by the natives to catch fish. We went out to the ocean, where, when we jumped in, we would be alone with one of the biggest, most beautiful creatures that I've ever seen. Now the whale shark is the size of a small school bus, but it's as gentle as a butterfly; it's probably the fish equivalent of a kind elephant.

As we're swimming around, laughing and playing, capturing videos, my grandma's still in the boat, smiling at us, because she couldn't swim. Still, she at least enjoyed being out in the ocean with the family. My dad was trying to swim, get a selfie, and take one for his vlogging channel. My mom was trying to take a picture to show off to her friends, who once made fun of her for having a son who dropped out of dental school. It felt peaceful to be with such a large creature and my family in that moment.

I remember thinking, *This is what eternity will feel like, as I hold it in the palm of my hand, for the rest of my life, as I hold it in the palm of my hand, for this hour, I will make sure to slow the time down, and not to think.* To look at my mom and remember how her face looked, with her radiant eyes and youthful face, and my dad, who was crying with joy as the whale shark accidentally touched him. Pete and Angelique were much better swimmers than I was. Pete had experience swimming in rivers and lakes back in his hometown in the UK, and he even taught me how to tread water, which, embarrassingly, I didn't know how to do.

I wanted to fully savor that moment as I rolled my grandma to the dinner table. It made me realize just how beautiful and important family truly is. When my uncle and his family joined us at the table, we held hands in prayer, expressing our gratitude to God for blessing us with one another, giving us the strength to overcome trauma, and nurturing the bonds that help us endure any suffering.

I looked at my grandma, who survived multiple strokes, faced numerous hardships, endured financial burdens, and experienced the death of her husband. I thought of my uncle, who had to assume the responsibilities of the household before he turned thirteen. I reflected on my dad, who sold items on the street to provide for his family when he was younger. I saw my mom, the woman who left behind the home she knew to build a new life in America with just $500 in her and my dad's account, all while trying to raise two kids. I thought of my aunt, who radiated joy and youthfulness. I looked at my sister, who experienced the struggles of surviving alone in Thailand with almost no money, and how she transformed her painful past into a beautiful life. I admired the laughter of my uncle's children and saw the kindness in Pete's eyes, which seemed to say, "I've seen a lot of pain in life, but I choose to soften my heart and give love to those around me."

I wondered how I could bottle up this feeling and hold it forever, or at least open it whenever I feel down, sad, depressed, or filled with anxiety. I wondered how my grandma could live so long, even after eating bread, sweets, and pork all the time. Or my uncle, who smoked and drank, yet he's one of the skinniest people that I know. He looked just as youthful as my dad, who didn't drink.

As I reflected on how close our family was, I began to realize the secret that I often overlooked when I chased better health to live long, look young, and stay young. That is family, and the bonds between them are the most essential things for living long and maintaining that childlike curiosity, playfulness, and energy. In Chinese culture, it's called *Xiào (shyow)*. It's the root of all virtue, the gentle duty to care for one's parents and honor one's lineage. Where intergenerational harmony is a biological and spiritual force that slows aging, restores balance, and anchors us to purpose by sharing meals, visiting elders, telling stories, and modeling respect, not as tradition, but as daily medicine. That's when I realized that *Xiào* isn't just obedience in Asian culture, but honor that heals both ways.

My uncle would tell me that in Confucian thought, *Xiào* (filial piety) is the most fundamental of all moral duties. This concept emphasizes a child's respect for their parents, an adult's care for their aging elders, and a person's gratitude towards their ancestors. Neglecting this duty is not merely considered immoral; it is believed to bring disorder into one's body, home, and society. He would say that "Chinese medicine sees the family as a system of *Qi*: When respect and love flow up the chain (from child to parent) and protection and wisdom flow down (from parent to child), the body and soul remain in rhythm. When this flow is broken (neglect, resentment, abandonment), stress accumulates. And stress, as we now know, accelerates aging." He would say this with a bottle of beer in his hand, ironically, as my dad started laughing, telling him to quit drinking and smoking. My uncle responded with a parable.

"There was once a man whose aging father came to live with him, his wife, and their young son. The old man's hands trembled. His eyesight faded. At dinner, he often spilled his rice and tea, and his mouth sometimes dripped soup. The wife grew irritated. The man, embarrassed by the mess and noise, took his father's meals away from the family table and made him eat in the kitchen, alone, from a wooden bowl to prevent breakage.

"One day, the man came home and saw his little boy in the corner, carving something with a piece of wood. 'What are you making, son?' he asked, kneeling beside him. The child looked up, smiling: 'I'm making a wooden bowl... for you. For when you're old like Grandpa.'

"The man froze. In that moment, he saw his own future and felt his father's shame. That night, he brought his father back to the table.

They gave him a warm cloth napkin. They let him spill without judgment. From then on, the boy watched them eat together, as a family."

Regardless of whether my uncle kept on drinking or not, I realized that what's more important is how you treat your aging parents while they are alive. And how your kids or future kids see you treating your parents as they age. The reason his kids treated my uncle and his wife so well was that, even though he had a vice of drinking, his kids saw him take care of his mom no matter what happened. As a result, the kids learned to be there for their parents.

My sister and I are so close with my parents because I see just how much my mom loves her mom, even though my grandma is hardheaded and stubborn at times, and rude and loud to people that she doesn't know. Our kids will treat us as we treat our parents. I had to learn this fast, as I had a bad relationship with my parents for nearly half a decade until I mustered up the strength to finally heal what was broken.

As our family gathered together to enjoy the generous spread of fish and rice set out before us, we shared the meal potluck-style. Everyone was eating with their hands, laughing, joking, and engaging in playful banter, much like our ancestors had done for thousands of years. It felt refreshing to experience this simple form of family bonding in a modern world that often complicates such moments. This feeling was my fountain of youth.

Recent research supports ancient Chinese wisdom by showing that strong family bonds are beneficial. They can lower stress and blood pressure. In addition, respected and involved grandparents often live longer, and children who feel connected to their parents have fewer chronic health issues as adults. Caring for elderly family members also improves mental health for both the older and younger generations. Moreover, storytelling helps protect brain function and emotional well-being, underscoring the lasting importance of family relationships. Family isn't just emotional; it's biological protection.

How the West Gets Family Wrong

Western View	Xiào View (Traditional)
Individualism	Interdependence
"Move out early"	"Care for your parents"
Retirement homes	Multigenerational homes
Freedom = separation	Freedom = belonging
Success = wealth	Success = filial virtue

Xiào isn't about being perfect. It's about being present.

Applying *Xiào* in Daily Life Without Guilt or Perfection:

➤ Call your parents.

➤ Ask them how they met.

➤ Cook their favorite meal.

➤ Visit your elders before it's too late.

➤ Share your childhood stories with your kids.

➤ Let your children see you honor your parents.

➤ Have them write in journals as a keepsake for their memories.

That modeling plants a seed of virtue deeper than any lesson.

Daily Habits to Practice *Xiào* (Filial Piety):

> ➤ Weekly family meals, with phones off.

> ➤ Storytelling nights, ask elders to tell their childhood tales.

> ➤ Record interviews with parents/grandparents.

> ➤ Teach your kids how to say "thank you" to elders properly.

> ➤ Speak with kindness even when stressed. Tone is legacy.

> ➤ Help with chores quietly, as they once helped you.

Youth fades where resentment grows, but it lingers in homes filled with warmth, laughter, and reverence. Every bowl washed. Every hug given. Every story told is a wrinkle reversed in the soul. In honoring where we come from, we slow the aging of where we're going. *Xiào* is not a duty. It is alchemy. The kind that turns love into longevity.

As I close the pages of this book, I tell my daughter what it means to die, but more importantly, I emphasize how vital it is to live life fully with the people we love. I've observed that the youngest-looking people are not necessarily the ones who appear young, but rather those who possess a youthful spirit and a certain lightness in their eyes. I pray that you maintain that lightness and remind yourself that life isn't about looking young, but about preserving the youthful, childlike spirit that has always been in your heart. I love you.

BEFORE YOU GO... A SMALL GIFT

Thank you for walking with me through these pages. Writing this book was my way of passing along the timeless wisdom and gentle practices that changed my own health and the health of my family. But real transformation isn't in reading once; it's in the daily rhythm of small choices.

To support you beyond this book, I've created a set of simple, printable resources you can keep close as daily reminders. They're completely free, just for readers like you.

Here's what you'll find inside:

➤ **Stress to Stillness Checklist:** A simple daily guide to move from tension to peace. Each step helps you release mental clutter, ground your body, and return to a state of calm focus.

➤ **The *Qi* Flow Tracker:** A mindful daily log that connects breath, movement, food, emotions, and rest to help you notice what truly fuels or drains your life force.

➤ **The Morning Ritual Journal:** A morning reflection journal template to center your energy, set your intention, and begin your day with purpose, balance, and quiet strength.

➤ **The Evening Return Journal:** A nightly journaling ritual to release the day, restore peace in your body, and invite deep, healing sleep.

You can download them here: **mikevestil.com/longevity-gifts**

(or scan the QR code below)

SCAN ME

Carry these with you. Share them if you'd like. They're meant to help you live the principles of this book, not in theory, but in practice. One sip of tea, one mindful breath, one simple choice at a time.

CAN I ASK YOU SOMETHING SMALL?

If this book has met you in a season where you've been thinking about your health, your aging, or your energy, and if even one page gave you hope, clarity, or a practical shift to feel lighter and younger again, would you take 60 seconds to share that with others?

Reviews aren't just stars on Amazon. They're little reminders for the next person searching for ways to feel better in their body, to stay vibrant as they age, and to find joy in simple practices that last a lifetime. Your words might be the exact encouragement they need to begin.

It doesn't have to be long. Just a sentence or two about what connected with you is enough.

You can simply scan the QR code below, or go to this link: **mikevestil.com/longevity-review**

SCAN ME

I read every single one, and your words mean more than you realize. Thank you for being part of this journey with me. With gratitude, Mike Vestil.

THE JOURNEY CONTINUES

If you've made it here, you've done more than finish a book. You've chosen a way of living. You chose slow over frantic. To breathe over rush. Tea over turmoil. You chose to honor the wisdom that youthfulness isn't a number; it's a rhythm.

Maybe this is the first time you let yourself pause, feel the morning sun on your face, bare feet on the ground, a simple meal shared without a screen. Maybe you felt the quiet relief of knowing that "looking young" begins with **living simply**: less noise, more nature; less forcing, more flow. The *Dào* calls it returning, back to what's real, back to what you can carry with peace.

I didn't write these pages to promise miracles. I wrote them to offer what steadied my own family: small, faithful practices anyone can do. A cup of green tea instead of another anxious scroll. A gentle walk after lunch. A few acupressure points before sleep. Storytelling at the table. Honoring elders. Laughing more, striving less. These are not hacks; they're homecomings.

If there's anything I hope you carry forward, it's this: You don't need extreme routines to feel alive. You don't need to fight your body to care for it. You don't need to chase youth; **you can cultivate it** with kindness, consistency, and gratitude. Peace belongs to you, too. Joy belongs to you, too.

This last page isn't an ending; it's a doorway. Keep going. Keep choosing the gentle path when the world shouts for more. Keep choosing presence over perfection, family over frenzy, breath over burnout. And when you stumble (we all do), return to the basics:

warm tea, clean water, a short walk, early sleep, a prayer of thanks, and a phone call to someone you love.

If these words helped you, pass them on. Somewhere, someone you care about is tired, stressed, and forgetting how good simple can feel. Your share might be the reminder they've been waiting for.

Remember this: God is not finished with you. Your story is not fragile; it's fertile. The cracks aren't disqualifications; they're where the light warms you back to life. When you forget, come back to these pages. Let them remind you: you are designed for renewal, made for peace, and never walking alone.

With gratitude and hope,

Mike Vestil

ABOUT THE AUTHOR

MIKE VESTIL

I'm not a doctor, scientist, or anti-aging "guru." I'm the firstborn son of an immigrant family, and for as long as I can remember, I watched the people I love sacrifice their health for survival. My mom worked overnight shifts in scrubs, running on fumes. My dad carried the weight of dreams deferred, stress showing up in his body before it ever reached his words. And I carried the silent fear that life had to be this way, that growing older meant breaking down.

But when my own body started sending warnings, ulcers, fatigue, stress-related illness, I realized that getting older didn't have to mean getting weaker. That there was another path hidden in plain sight: the timeless wisdom of cultures that had quietly practiced health and vitality for centuries.

Inspired by ancient Chinese traditions and the lessons of my own family, I began studying the small, daily practices that add up to a long, happy, healthy life. Breathing. Walking. Eating in rhythm with nature and protecting peace as fiercely as we chase success. I discovered that longevity isn't found in miracle pills or expensive treatments, but in rituals, balance, and how we live the ordinary days.

Now I live simply in Asia, building a life around family, faith, and freedom. I've learned that real youthfulness isn't about erasing wrinkles or chasing perfection; it's about staying vibrant enough to be present for the people you love, decade after decade.

This book is for anyone who wants more than years on a calendar. It's for those who want energy that lasts, joy that lingers, and relationships that grow stronger as time goes on. It's for people who want to look young, stay young, and live long. Not just in body, but in spirit.

I don't write this as an expert looking down from a podium, but as someone still learning, still practicing, still walking this path every day. These pages are part story, part map. They're my way of saying: youth is not lost, it's lived. And it can still be yours.

Stay connected:

mikevestil.com: writings, reflections, and occasional updates

Instagram: @mikevestil